THE SUBTLETY OF BULLYING

Legal stuff:

THE AUTHOR AND PUBLISHER HAVE MADE THEIR BEST EFFORTS TO PRODUCE A HIGH QUALITY, INFORMATIVE AND HELPFUL VEHICLE. BUT THEY MAKE NO REPRESENTATION OR WARRANTIES OF ANY KIND WITH REGARD TO THE COMPLETENESS OR ACCURACY OF THE CONTENTS. THEY DO NOT ADVOCATE OR SUGGEST OR MAKE RECOMMENDATIONS OF ANY KIND AND ACCEPT NO LIABILITY OF ANY KIND FOR ANY LOSSES OR DAMAGES CAUSED OR ALLEGED TO BE CAUSED, DIRECTLY OR INDIRECTLY, FROM USING THE INFORMATION OR MATERIALS FOUND WITHIN

THE SUBTLETY OF BULLYING

Is bullying and intimidation a natural and necessary function of animal societies?

By

Ted Moss

A Book In The

Series Of Social Commentary

THE SUBTLETY OF BULLYING

All Rights Reserved © eam 2021

DEDICATION

This book is dedicated to the memory of Christopher Paul Wilson BA (Hons) Arch (13th July 1974–09th July 2018). A kind and gentle young man as evidenced by testimony of many friends, grateful for his help through dark times. A Liverpool lad by birth, this intelligent Scouser emigrated to the West Country in 1986 with mum and dad and siblings. After graduation, Christopher joined his dad in the family Building Design Business, which he took over around thirty months ago when his dad retired. However, sadly for everybody who knew him, Christopher left this world, days before his 44th Birthday.

AUTHOR'S NOTE

The concept of bullying, intimidation, coercion or whatever one wants to call being forced to do something against one's will is a subtext that runs through all of my books in the Unpalatable Truth series and in fact, runs throughout all of our lives and nobody appears to be exempt. Being ordered about by the boss or receiving a demand to pay money are everyday examples of being bullied, which my gentle reader will no doubt accept, but how about Time or Seasons? These are not generally thought of as sources of intimidation, however, if you don't do something before a certain time...

...you will lose something or you will not benefit or you will be forced to pay more.

If a farmer doesn't act fast enough when bad weather threatens...

...he or she will lose the harvest and will be unable to pay bills and might lose the farm.

The Earth itself is using Time and Weather to intimidate us. However, in this instance, the coercion is a warning for our species to act now to save all livings things from annihilation. The media has alerted us to global warming (supported by the scientific community) and we are aware of land erosion due to rising seas and icecaps melting and we know if we don't stop doing things that are causing that global warming now, future generations will suffer the consequences.

We have to accept we are reliant on world leaders to prevent the Earth from passing the point of no return. However, there are things we do not have to accept and this book is attempting to confront all manner of bullying head-on. First by recognising it, then unmasking it and finally finding ways to tackle it. However, things that appear to be bullying might not be bullying and we have to distinguish between them.

Definition Of Bullying

[…] Bullying is the use of force, coercion, or threat, to abuse, aggressively dominate or intimidate. The behaviour is often repeated and habitual. One essential prerequisite is the perception of an imbalance of physical or social power. This imbalance distinguishes bullying from conflict.

[…] Bullying is a subcategory of aggressive behaviour characterised by the following three criteria: hostile intent, perceived imbalance of power, and repetition over a period of time.

[…] Bullying is the activity of repeated, aggressive behaviour intended to hurt another individual, physically, mentally, or emotionally or a combination of all three […] *https://en.wikipedia.org/wiki/Bullying*

Definition Of Non-Academic Discipline

[…] Discipline in this sense is behaviour regulated to be in accordance with a particular system of governance, commonly applied to regulating human and animal behaviour to its society or environment […] *https://en.wikipedia.org/wiki/discipline*

PREFACE

The thing many people don't appreciate about bullying is that issues can lay dormant until an event, it can be something seemingly quite innocuous, awakens in the psyche, a distant trauma with unpleasant consequences; and that is what happened to this writer. A bad experience that I was convinced I had dealt with 50 plus years ago, returned, right out of the shadows to haunt my every waking thought.

A woman, around 30 stone, yelling in the foulest of language for people to move out of her way because she was disabled drove a four-wheel, invalid scooter over my foot; it was painful. I swear the machine would have towed a caravan with not a great deal of difficulty! I don't know what came over me, but I had the greatest of urges to scream at her that I was born with a malformed chest causing me to have difficulties breathing, but I didn't go around swearing at people. The condition was then called a *Depressed Sternum*, now it is known as a *Pectus Excavatum*, which is Latin. I state this not to mock, but to acknowledge that members of professions, such as Medicine, the Law and Horticulture, for example, will use Latin to overcome language barriers.

As the condition progressed my deformed rib cage caused my heart and lungs to be depressed resulting in me having difficulty breathing. Because a depressed sternum is not obvious like a missing limb or a disfigurement nobody knew about my condition and I never told anybody.

Being forever out of breath, I had no interest in anything earning me the labels of being stupid and lazy. I was late for everything or avoided it entirely, much preferring to stay in bed, which later in life I realised had quite dark connotations, as I would often hunch myself into the foetus position and wish I could stay that way forever, fuelling the part of the accusation that considered me to be a lazy child.

In school, I was made to play football and although I gave of my best, being constantly breathless, I couldn't always run fast enough to intercept the ball, often resulting in our team losing and blaming me. I never defended myself preferring to take the blame and enduring the 'silent treatment' and the odd beating sooner than admit I was a *freak*; which caused me to *hate football.* And as my father, my brother, cousins and uncles were all football fans I think in disliking the game I was a big disappointment as a son to my father.

My father has been gone these 30 years past and I feel disloyal saying these things now, but it is now, as I am nearing the end of my own life that I have gathered the courage to speak about my unpleasant school days.

The fact that I was also partially deaf in my left ear, which caused me to miss much of what was said in class (because I would not wear my state-supplied hearing aid, because my classmates thought it was hilarious to pull it out of my ear, which hurt), added to the accusation of me being thought of as stupid.

During an employment medical at age 17 the chest condition was noted and I underwent a series of operations to correct matters. Initially, my chest was opened first to break and reset my deformed ribs, which were screwed to a metal plate to secure while they set in the proper position. Around 18 months later I had another operation to adjust the metal plate to allow for chest expansion as I grew and the plate was removed completely in a further operation about 12 months after that.

Although the operations were successful in achieving the objective of righting my deformed chest, I inherited a number of negative issues. I was left with a weak chest wall, a protruding rib cage, causing me constant difficulties and lasting damage to my heart, which manifests in irregular heartbeats and for which I need daily medication to control the rhythm.

In addition, I have inherited what is known as gynaecomastia, also referred to as 'man boobs', something I was warned might happen as a result of the series of operations cutting through the chest and severely compromising the pectoral muscles. These issues troubled me for years and I thought I had, at last, come to terms with them, but the incident with the woman in the invalid scooter brought back the painful memories of the *bullying* and the operations and the names I was called and that is why I am writing about *bullying* in all of its horrible forms. With regard to the hearing problem, I developed strategies and learned to live with it.

Today hearing aids are almost invisible, but in the 1960s they were an unwieldy and complicated affair and not at all child friendly. The equipment I had to wear consisted of an earpiece, connected by a wire to a sound collecting device, about the size of a twenty packet of cigarettes that needed to be fixed to the front of the body in such a way that it was not obscured by clothing. A further wire connected it to a battery pack within a leather case, around the size of a small camera, which hung at the side from a leather strap. In the event my gentle reader is interested, illustrations can be found on the Internet.

February 2021   *Ted Moss*

CONTENTS

CONTENTS

ACKNOWLEDGEMENTS

Images and illustrations in this book are mostly courtesy of https://pixabay.com an international free-to-use website for sharing photos, illustrations, and graphics and when befitting I have credited other sources. However, despite my best efforts this has not always been possible. Therefore, should one discover a vehicle lacking appropriate acknowledgement, I apologise and suggest advising my publisher will see full credit given in future editions.

STAND ALONE NOVELS

The Ten Percent Man
ISBN: 978-1-4452-7322-8 Paperback
ISBN: 978-1-4457-1566-7 Hardback

The Laird Of Glendawn
ISBN 978-1-4092-0586-9 Paperback
ISBN 978-1-4457-1580-3 Hardback

UNPALATABLE TRUTHS

Are Gods A Fabrication Of The Mind Of Man?
ISBN 978-1-7166-4600-3 Paperback

Homelessness Is Escalating Year After Year – Why?
ISBN 978-1-7165-8872-3 Paperback

The Festive Season Naughty Or Nice?
ISBN 978-1-7164-3513-3 Paperback

The European Union
Should We Stay Or Should We Go?
ISBN 978-1-716-39515-4 Paperback

The Subtlety Of Bullying
ISBN 978-1-68474-151-9 Paperback

**FUTURE TITLES IN THE UNPALATABLE
TRUTH SERIES ARE PLANNED**

THE SUBTLETY OF BULLYING

Is bullying and intimidation a bad or not such a bad thing that might teach the human species valuable lessons about itself?

That might appear to be a strange, even a callous thing to say. However, a closer look at the whole subject of bullying reveals some important lessons that we, as a species, would do well to take notice of and learn from.

To make the point I have written a verse about Bullying that will be found at the end of this book. The points I make, both in these pages and in the verse, did not come about overnight; the concept of bullying has been a major part of my life. My gentle reader will be aware of the bullying as a consequence of my disability, however, I feel that has heightened my senses, causing me to be more cognisant of the subtlety of bullying generally.

I have been watching and listening to the speeches of various governments since I was a little lad (there was nothing wrong with the brain, it was the body that let me down).

I came from a staunch Labour household, all socialists, although my dad bought the Daily Mail and said
if he was wealthy he would vote for the Conservative
party.

Even as a naive little chap I could
not understand how anybody could
hold two such fundamentally oppos-
ing views at the same time. I be-
lieved that the advantaged had a duty
to help the disadvantaged and although a lot has happened to me
since I was a child, my views have
never changed nor will they ever.

Despite a number of negative issues, as previously
mentioned, I managed to get a university degree. Now
it is not my intention to downplay the hard work we
all put into studying for our degrees. However, when
we strip away the mortarboard and gown we have a
piece of paper confirming that at a particular time the
holder was able to regurgitate random pieces of information that she or he had spent a number of years
learning; but that doesn't last.

It's some years since I graduated and now I struggle
to answer questions on psychology and related sub-
jects on University Challenge. But it doesn't really
matter what degree one reads for as everybody learns
an extremely important thing in higher education, one
might say acquires an important skill that lasts a life-
time.

One learns to think for oneself – to accept nothing and to question everything until it has been proved. To look beneath the 'Newspeak' as Eric *George Orwell* Blair would have put it and dig-out and expose the truth. And if the actual truth isn't immediately recognisable then to recognise that something is not quite right. For me, that meant a return to contradictory thoughts of my past such as Labour and the Daily Mail, Socialist to Conservative and I recognised what was going on and that was intimidation. Or to remove any pleasant references and give it its proper title we are talking about, *bullying*!

I accept that when I was a child I was ignorant of the political process and could not have had the knowledge to form a political opinion, but as a thinking individual things were different and I knew whatever I was it certainly was not a Liberal anti-pluralist; this time my conviction was not based in ignorance but, on experience.

I had witnessed the hatchet job that Thatcher and her mentor Milton Friedman and his Chicago school of economic theory inflicted on this country and I recognised the cruel philosophy that Capitalism is built upon – again one of *bullying*! To this, my gentle reader might argue that Capitalism brings us the essentials, even the good things of life at acceptable prices such as food, cars, houses, furniture, tools, coffee and toys for example and of course this is right, but at what price? One only receives these things whilst the Capitalist's production process is making profits, when production stops or slows, profits stop, the good things stop naturally as a consequence and people, perhaps you gentle reader, are thrown out of work as factories are resited in third world countries where the capitalist can get somebody to do your job for a fraction of the wage bill with no thought whatsoever for your welfare, *think...*

*...moving pro**D**uction of **Y**our famous **S**uction device abr**O**ad, making hundreds redu**N**dant at home.*

In this instance one might feel that the natural course of Capitalism and its philosophy of cruel bullying is built upon Nature, perhaps relying on Charles Darwin's observations of the Survival of the Fittest for proof. In reply, I would suggest that is not the case and that Nature and Capitalism work on two different plains and that Capitalism is far and away the more sinister of the two.

In response, my gentle reader might say that the foregoing is just my opinion and argue that on the face of it Capitalism mimicking nature for a cruel bullying model to follow is a compelling idea particularly when the herd abandons the Wildebeest baby to die and the Antelope apparently brutally assaults her young fawn. However, I would still argue against nature being cruel and that Nature works on strict unyielding discipline, not cruelty.

The foregoing remarks will be better appreciated when we understand that the Wildebeest baby was severely deformed, could not walk and would prevent the herd from reaching the next waterhole, thereby bringing about the demise of the whole herd. This is an example *of doing that, which is for the benefit of the many* and in psychology, it is known as Utilitarianism. My gentle reader might wish to read about the work of Jeremy Bentham (1748 – 1832).

As for the assault, which the fawn received, the reason for this apparent cruelty was for wandering off, away from the safe care of its mother. The pain of being struck by its mother was nothing compared to the pain it would have endured by wondering into the jaws of a pride of lions. This was not cruelty, but strict and necessary discipline, an example of Operant Conditioning.

There is a theory within psychology, which postulates we are all motivated by the concept of *punishment or reward*. Meaning we avoid something if it will hurt (punish) us and we do something if it will gratify (reward) us. All of the above comes under the umbrella term of Behaviourism. Again my gentle reader might wish to view authority on the subject of Behaviourism and Operant conditioning by reading BF Skinner (1904 – 1990).

I feel that the constructs of Utilitarianism and Operant Conditioning along with other schools of thought within psychology such as, Classical Conditioning and Psychodynamics together with therapies such as Rogerian and Aversion in collaboration with the teachings of nature are extremely fascinating and offer positive lessons for mankind. Yet whilst deep in the process of intellectualising ourselves out of existence, our species has chosen to ignore them, in my view, at our peril; the consequences of which society is beginning to experience.

From the foregoing, we glean that the whole of nature is grounded in a philosophy that might seem like cruelty and bullying, but in reality is the manifestation of an innate strict and unyielding discipline, essential for the protection of lower animals to ensure the survival of the species.

Whereas, the whole of humanity is grounded in a philosophy that might be touted as a discipline but is in fact based on cruelty, intimidation and *bullying* in the higher animal order, which most children first come to experience in their school life but, it doesn't stop there.

Being coerced is so prevalent in society that we accept it as part of life and don't even see it as bullying. So much so in fact that bullying might be seen as a natural part of our progress through life, preparing us for greater and harsher intimidation and coercion and out and out *bullying* later in life.

I feel this notion of bullying to be such an important concept – that we need to grasp and fully recognise coercion and intimidation in all of its many ugly and stealthy forms and the disguises it can assume.

Today's modern forms of technology are wonderful and far in advance of anything our forefathers could have imagined. We have the Internet and social media and within a few seconds anybody with a connection can send and receive messages around the world, either by text, email or by a method of telephone and video. However, these wonders have their dark side and have enabled others to groom and bully young people in the comparative safety of their own homes, which, sadly has led to suicide.

As I think back I realise that my father's skewed view of Socialism was not of his making; once again bullying was at work here. My father's newspaper, the Daily Mail, although Capitalist owned and, therefore Tory, appealed to working people due to the style of its editorials and the nature of its stories, which skilfully misdirected or conveniently overlooked relevant news to curry favour with the workers.

This is seductive brainwashing, which it and other newspapers still practice today together with some alternative forms of the Fourth Estate and which we shall now examine closely.

BULLIED BY WAY OF THE FOURTH ESTATE

Returning to the Daily Mail, this is the newspaper associated with Jonathan Harold Esmond Vere Harmsworth. I'll call him Jonny Harmsworth, I think I heard of a title knocking about, but, I don't recognise that outmoded, anachronistic nonsense.

Harmsworth inherited the organ from pater, who got it from his daddy and little Jonny together with one-time editor Paul Michael (no! not that one this is Paul Michael Dacre, who I understand was known to Geordie Greig and the rest of his enemies in the DMG as: 'DADDY DAYCARE', which I understand he hated) used the newspaper to discredit any socialist ideas.

Things are never straight forward these days in anything and it is difficult to know who is pulling the strings at the Daily Mail as I understand that a Jewish chap by the name of Guy Zitter is the Managing Director of the Tory-supporting rag.

Generally, the Daily Mail along with the rest of the Tory press seemed obsessed with putting all of its resources into doing a hatchet job on the Labour party. However, due to the Covid-19 pandemic, these newspapers are having to put all efforts into supporting their hapless Tory leader.

Although the 'man who would be king' has achieved his ambition, it is probably at about the worst time since the Bubonic Plague of the 17th century. Many people have been heard to say they dislike Boris Johnson due to the mixed and contradictory messages coming out of the office of the Prime Minister. And although the Labour party lost the last election the party members are probably having soothing thoughts of a visible mass of condensed watery vapour resplendent with a highly polished silver interior.

Pre-2020 the Tory press was having a right old go at Jeremy Corbyn and because Jeremy did not own his own newspaper he could not fight back. Figuratively speaking it was as if Jeremy was hog-tied with hands behind his back, the rope around his neck and tied to his feet so if he moved he would strangle himself.

That is what the Tory media machine appeared to be doing to Jeremy; is that fair? No, it certainly is not, but why was the Tory press taking such a position against Jeremy Corbyn? Well before we look at the why first let us look at the how.

When I look at Jeremy Corbyn I see a not very impressive gentleman who is not particularly concerned with his dress presentation and appears to be in need of a shave. Of course, I accept that looks are not the man and I can see through this image to an intelligent Socialist who advocated reversing austerity cuts to public services and welfare funding and proposed renationalisation of public utilities and the railways. In short Jeremy Corbyn appeared to care for people.

"What kind of city are we living in, if we encourage the development or ownership of large, expensive properties for investment and land banking... while people are sleeping on the streets?" Jeremy Bernard Corbyn (born 26 May 1949) MP, Leader of the Labour Party and of the Opposition 2015 – 2019.

Regardless, of Jeremy's politics, I am far too aware that the brain is not the first thing that the young, modern electorate recognises in politicians. And as Jeremy stood for everything the Tories do not want the constant bad press that Jeremy was getting from the Conservative-supporting Fourth Estate was a sign they were terrified of him getting elected. And I fear, because of his appearance Jeremy offered himself up to the Tory press to be ridiculed as indeed was the case with Michael Foot.

Unable to find fault with Michael Foot the politician, the Tory-controlled media ridiculed Michael Foot the man because of the way he dressed, satirising the appearance of arguably one of this country's greatest thinkers and a champion of socialism.

"As for any insoluble economic problems that may arise if the top is deprived of their initiative, I would answer 'To hell with them.' The top is greedy and mean and will always find a way to take care of themselves. They always do." Michael Mackintosh Foot FRSL (23 July 1913 – 3 March 2010)

Michael was more concerned with people than sartorial elegance and was often seen out and about in casual attire, presenting an easy target for the lowly and cowardly attacks he received. The sad thing was that the majority, foolish arm of the working class fell for it and  Michael Foot was judged more on his appearance rather than his wonderful brain and socialist ideals.

The above was an example of the way governments treat adversaries by mocking, satirising or just humiliating them. In the next chapter, we witness a far worse strategy, that of 'demonising'.

So why would the Mail together with other right-wing newspapers and their webpages take such a furious position against Jeremy? One explanation is that we were seeing a barometer of feeling betraying fear. Could it be they were running scared, did they feel that Jeremy presented a credible challenge to the nest of vipers? The following piece from Private Eye magazine would seem to suggest yes, they did:

"The Integrity Initiative, ostensibly a campaign against 'Russian disinformation' faced Labour Party anger and a Foreign Office inquiry when it emerged recently that the supposedly 'independent' initiative was backed by £2m of government money and had been circulating anti-Jeremy Corbyn articles." Private Eye, Issue No 1486 22nd December 2018 to 10th January 2019, page 11, Hot News, Cold War.

Apparently, the information came to light when documents leaked by hacktivist group *Anonymous* in November 2018 revealed that the Integrity Initiative received the money from the Foreign Office in 2017/18. This was eventually confirmed by an embarrassed Alan Duncan, Foreign Office minister. To digress for a moment:

Whether or not the electorate was aware of the above, I feel the people who might have supported Jeremy Corbyn lost any faith they might have had in him (and fell victim to the Tory election smokescreen of getting out of Europe) when he insulted democracy by stating he would support a second referendum on Britain's membership of The European Union.

This from a man who would have known that joining the EU and relinquishing our sovereignty (right to self-government) was disloyal in the first instance. Therefore, supporting moves that might reverse that lawful and correcting first referendum's decision by the British people is tantamount to criminality.

The above was not the reason Jeremy Corbyn was stood down from his position in the Labour party, for that we need to return to the media to understand why and who caused Jeremy Corbyn to be no longer the leader of the Labour party.

Essentially, an extremely powerful entity able to intimidate world affairs caused the fall of Corbyn and might even have completely destroyed his political life for all time and that powerful entity was the so-called State of Israel.

Jeremy Corbyn had been accused of being anti-Semitic and was compared to the late right-wing Tory MP Enoch Powell, which Jeremy asserted was "hurtful," "quite offensive" and "bey- ond excessive".

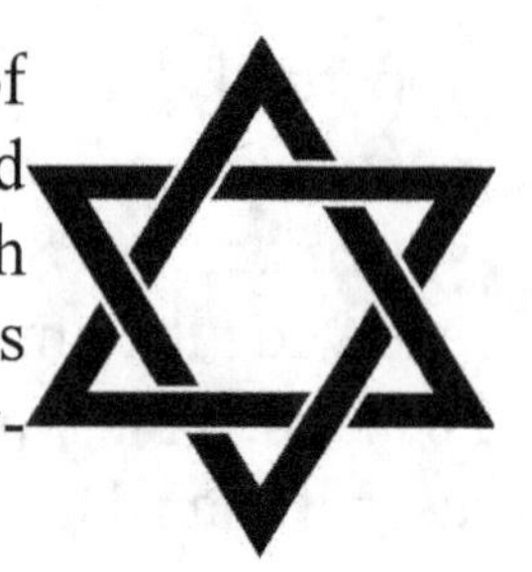

Despite Corbyn denying meaning to be offensive and stating that he had spent his life exposing racism in all its ugly forms, the majority-owned and or controlled Jewish media in the United Kingdom kept up a relent- less campaign until the Labour party suspended him.

Am I prejudiced against Jews? Probably, for as an Atheist I am prejudiced against all religionists and their beliefs, however, what we are discussing here has nothing to do with beliefs, but facts. I am pointing out that Jeremy Corbyn's accuser's claims were the subjective opinions of *one man*, entirely unsupported. Whereas my remarks can be completely supported. "Six Jewish companies own 96% of the World's me- dia" https://en.wikipedia.org/wiki

That is a start, but my remarks made at the protest of the *bullying* of Jeremy Corbyn concerned Jewish owned and or controlled media in the United Kingdom, so let us take a look at those companies and their parent or subsidiary businesses. We will begin with TV, Radio and Satellite Broadcasting:

BBC television controlled by Alan Yentob, ITV, subsidiary of Carlton Communications, controlled by Michael Green; Granada plc controlled by Steve Morrison; BSkyB controlled by Rupert Murdoch; all of BBC radio is controlled by Jenny Abramsky. That is a selection of Jewish media over the airwaves, now we move on to Jewish owned or controlled newspapers.

The Daily and Sunday Express together with The Daily Star, Northern and Shell company, owned by Richard Desmond.

Incidentally, Private Eye magazine calls, Richard Desmond Dirty Des because he made (and by all accounts still makes) a fortune selling pornography.

Sunday EXPRESS

Get you daily dose of Excrement from the newspaper that is what it is

Rupert Murdoch owns News International, which owns the Times, Sunday Times and the Sun; the Telegraph Group owned by Hollinger International Inc, all owned by Conrad Black who now owns the Daily Telegraph, the Sunday Telegraph and the Spectator magazine and many other newspapers around the world; and of course, Jonny Harmsworth and his rag, which although not Jewish owned appears to be controlled by a Jewish chap these days.

I think that should be enough to cause my gentle readers' minds to begin to process the above information and understand why and *how* Jeremy Corbyn was subjected to a mass besmirching campaign by an extremely powerful organisation.

That is bullying, intimidation, coercion and any other label one can think of in the extreme and is frightening as it demonstrates the power of the media and the damage it can generate supporting *one individual's subjective opinion.* A Rabbi's view *not fact,* supported by the members of the huge organisation that he heads, causes its machine to bring about the destruction of a man's career; a man who just happened to be *influential in the people's political party.*

This writer has learned much as I have gone through life. At one time I was of the opinion that religionism, people believing in their giant Supernatural anthropomorphic God creature, was the problem. I have since changed my understanding and I now realise that is not the problem. The problem is believing and *bullying* others into believing that your Supernatural, anthropomorphic God creature and belief system is better than everybody else's – it causes wars.

It's not the little people who cause the trouble, it's the big guys whether Jews, Catholics, Muslims Sikhs, etc or non-believers. If there is money to be made they will go for it either alone, or if profits demand, they will climb into bed together without giving a second thought or care for the possibility of potential consequences for people; for example, think of a well-known bank and its connection to fraud, money laundering, gunrunning and drug smuggling, which was apparently too big to prosecute.

Michael Foot called those who care only for money, THE TOP. We should always remember the crux of Michael's words: [...] *The top is greedy and mean and will always find a way to take care of themselves. They always do* [...] Let us return to the little people.

The little people might be small in stature and bank-balance, but I have always found them to be big hearted, honest, helpful and generous and if personal experience is anything to go by that includes Jewish people.

In my life I have known two Jewish people, one was a boss and the other was introduced to me by a friend. Both of these people were comparative strangers to me, in that they knew next to nothing about my private life or who my family were and I only knew them from work and a third party, and yet both of them went out of their way to help me without asking anything in return.

Anti-Bullying

As this book is all about bullying I think anything we can say that helps prevent bullying or gives ideas for things that assist people and their lives and not constantly drains people of their energy and the will to live has got to be a good thing. Therefore, I feel that the following is appropriate to be mentioned in my book.

When we got to know each other a little better one of my new friends, Steven told me a story about the little Jew. A story with a lesson and a message that we would all do well to note and emulate. It has nothing to do with bullying, in fact, quite the opposite, we might call it helping our fellow woman, man or even *anti-bullying*, now there is a nice title and which is a welcome change.

Steven said to me: "Let's suppose that a chap found himself, all alone in the middle of a park hungry and naked, in the early hours of the morning, what would he do?" He saw the puzzlement on my face and said: "Come on, just humour me, what would he do?"

I replied: "I don't know, never thought about it. I suppose he would soon be picked up by the police or he might make his way to the police station..." "...Whereupon he would either be told to sod off or would be charged with indecency," said Steven, finishing off my sentence. "I suppose," I replied, to which Steven responded:

"If he was a Jew he would make his way to the Jewish part of the city and knock on the door of the first Jewish business he came upon. He would be welcomed with open arms and clothed, fed and given a bed for the night. The next day, having been informed of the chap's presence, a council made up of the local Jewish businesspeople would convene and interrogate him.

"If he had a trade they would set him up in business, providing premises and whatever tools and/or stock was needed to make the business work, either from member's own possessions or buying them and asking nothing more than the replacement of stock provided and a reasonable rate of interest on the return of all monies expended and reasonable rent for the premises. Then Jews from miles around would be informed and would give the chap their business." Steven continued,

"If he had no trade they would have him employed in one of the member's businesses, where he would be taught a trade," said Steven and seeing me smiling he smiled and added:

"Of course had the non-Jewish chap known this, he too would have been helped in the same way, we are not all money-mad. We want what most people want and that is to be able to live our lives in peace and quiet, free of trouble. To enjoy the company of our family and friends and to love our kids. As for business, we ask for a reasonable return on investment, which is not asking too much don't you think?"

What would my gentle reader reply to that question? Beginning with absolutely nothing and being set up in business with everything required to make the business a success. Then repaying any monies at a reasonable rate of interest and a fair rent for the premises to the good people who made it all possible for you, I don't think it is asking too much and causes me to think how we all might do the same to help those not as fortunate. And in fact, in regard to people helping people, my ancestors appear to have enjoyed a similar experience, although I did not learn of it for many years; and of which I shall explain in detail presently.

When I was growing up my father and mother went to work, but my mother also found time to do the housework. There was no touching or hugging in our family, which I think was the norm in the 1950s as my friends' families seemed pretty much the same. It was called the 'Old School' mentality, meaning you didn't show your emotions, but kept things bottled up and you didn't ask for help (as it was seen as a sign of weakness), but stood on your own two feet, as it was called. This philosophy, I now recognise, was a hidden form of bullying.

The working class always had it hard and complained amongst themselves, but they never complained to the boss for fear of losing their jobs. This attitude was brought into the home and we were brought up to believe that *children should be seen and not heard.*

My father was the very epitome of the 'Old School', he never asked for help from anybody, he kept to himself and although he had been in the Second World War he never spoke about the war or about family history or showed any emotion... that is... until he was on his death bed.

It was in the Liverpool hospital that he gripped my arm tightly attempting to pull me close and I assisted his extreme effort. My father was in a guards regiment during the Second World War and he was a big man over 6 foot in height and weighing over 17 stone. The thin man in the bed, dying of acute Myeloid Leukaemia was skin and bones and weighed a fraction of his usual weight; I know, as I had often carried him to the toilet on the odd time he was allowed home.

I had been stuck in traffic and arrived at the hospital as everybody else was either leaving or had left. Seeing me hurrying, out of breath, the Ward Sister told me that she was going on her break and I could sit with my father until she returned.

My father's eyes watered as he mentioned a place I had never heard of, Peenemünde. He continued to tell a story of his regiment marching into this place in Germany and releasing dying slaves from a concentration camp at which point he began crying.

I have since discovered that Peenemünde was the production plant for the V1 (known as the Doodlebug) and later, the V2, unmanned jet propelled explosive rockets, manufactured by Germany and used to bomb British towns and cities and the slaves were people who were worked to death in the production process.

He said the Moses Family came from Hungry just before the turn of the 18th century. I thought my old man was losing his grip on reality, "what the heck was he talking about?" And then he said, "*...they changed the name!*"

Anglicised

The following is relevant to the concept of *Anti-Bullying* and also in order to expand on what was said earlier about the little people helping each other. Towards the end of his life, my father told me of a conversation he had had with his father.

He revealed to me that the antecedents of our family were Jewish people called Moses who had come to England, around 1780, which might have been to escape persecution, but he couldn't be sure. He said they had settled in Holborn in London where a great relation had helped the family set up their tailoring business.

Over a century later, due to a gathering climate of hostility towards Jewish people, the family name was anglicised by removing the 'e' and family members began moving away.

I understand that some might have emigrated to Australia, some to the Americas, some to Ireland, but our branch of the family stayed in the country and moved to Lancashire; and my father also told me an amazing thing, which was supported by my mother.

One of his brothers had invented the invisible mending process for repairing clothing.

DIRECT STATE BULLYING
Lies & Demonising

When caught out in some trickery or attempting to hide it before it is discovered, a pet ploy of governments is to use the Jester or the Devil tactic – meaning they either mock or demonise would-be detectors. In the last chapter, we saw an example of mocking by the way the Tory press treated Michael Foot and how Jeremy Corbyn's presentation would mark him out for similar treatment. In this chapter, we shall take a look at an example of the Devil approach and see how this demonising tactic creates scaremongering amongst the populace, by scapegoating, an individual, a group or a thing.

Often this is done so subtlety as to not recognise it is happening, whereas other times it is glaringly obvious. Such an example was the way Thatcher's Tory Government treated the coal miners' legitimate dispute with the head of the (NCB) National Coal Board, Ian MacGregor, the American multimillionaire butcher of the British Steel Industry, that turned into the Coal Miners' strike during the 12 month period from March 1984–through to March 1985.

The 1984-85 miners' strike was the lengthiest, most bitter national strike in British working-class history. In an effort to defend their jobs and lifestyle, for 12 months the miners fought an unparalleled battle against the full might of Thatcher, her mentor Milton Friedman and his Chicago School of economics.

The power of the Tory press machine went to work against the miners poisoning the minds of the weak, would-be, socialists of the day and winning them over with right-wing vitriolic messages, *demonising, and scapegoating the miners as being troublemakers.*

Apparently, the Thatcher Government was not averse to helping matters along as information leaked over the years since the strike suggests that trouble makers were indeed within the ranks of the miners. However, they were not from the mining community, but MI5 plants, put there by the Tories to cause mayhem by fighting with the police causing the police to retaliate with extreme prejudice.

People who used to think: 'our policemen are wonderful' were shocked into reality when nightly the television graphically depicted violent attacks and aggressive assaults by police officers beating-up, hurting and maiming good and honest working people.

With the Government under the influence of the Chicago School, our uniformed police presented as automatons, seeming only too ready to do the bidding of their masters regardless of what that might be. And from what we saw of their actions during the miner's strike that could very well be torture and murder. If my gentle reader doubts this I would recommend investigating the countries where the Chicago School practised its dark arts.

Countries such as Indonesia, Brazil Argentina and Chile and latterly Iraq. Those countries were bullied into submission and left with raging inflation and high prices. High unemployment has run amok in those countries causing the death and suffering of millions of people as roaming police death squads, together with the military, tortured and murdered those who opposed them.

Should my gentle reader still be of the opinion that these things could never happen in England's Green and Pleasant Lands (even knowing how the miners were treated), then I would advise adding the Peterloo massacre of 1819 to your list of investigations.

Of course, we have and need the detectives who investigate murders and rapes and bring the guilty to justice. However, it is the uniformed personnel of whom I speak who did themselves no favours in their treatment of the miners as the sheer *will* of the miners inspired the country – and people got behind them and gave unparalleled amounts of practical support in terms of money, clothing and food.

Furious at the support the people were giving the miners the bullying Conservative Government was determined to destroy the miners and in its fury it perpetrated what must be the most disgraceful action by any government against its people. The Conservative Government under the direction of Thatcher used the withdrawal of social security benefits. as a weapon against innocent babies in an effort to force their grandfathers, fathers, uncles and brothers to surrender the cause; in effect, the Government threw everything at the men.

A government led by a woman who had shown her spiteful colours years before by inventing a process to fleece children of ice-cream and then to rob them of school milk, as me and kids of my generation used to proclaim: "Maggie *Thatcher The Milk Snatcher!"*

Thatcher and her Government treated the miners as if they had committed treason and had puppet magistrates prosecute them. Nearly 10,000 hard-working people, who risked their lives to keep us warm every day of their working lives, were arrested. The puppet Magistrates and their puppet Courts were kept full of business by the actions of sycophantic Chief Constables.

Chief Constables who gave orders to police officers to subdue the strikers, apparently not caring how it was done and turning a blind eye to violent behaviour on the part of the police. Behaviour that savagely oppressed men fighting in the vanguard of a war against a transparently avaricious government resolved to crush the power of the united men and therefore Unions in general.

The Miners Ask For Help

All of that seemingly impossible to survive bullying, intimidation, police brutality and torture (police horses being ridden into people and walking on them), wasn't what beat the miners. What beat the miners were organisations that the members had paid into, week in, week out for years to help them during times of distress.

It is thought that the Miners should have won and sent Thatcher packing as besides having determination the miners had the support of the majority of the people of the country and would have beaten Thatcher if it had not been for trusted parties actively destabilising strike activity, working against the Miners.

The war and *it was a war, people died* was going the way of the miners a number of times. Yet when the miners called upon trusted parties for help, they were shown the door. And all the time the miners were struggling against the *bullies* in Government the NUM failed to support them with a ballot for a national strike.

And when the Miners asked the TUC for help, no help came from that quarter. Neither the NUM nor the TUC would stick their necks out to really do something to help the working class struggle against a harsh Government in the most protracted national trade strike in history but still, the miners persevered. And seeing the resolve in ordinary people a shocked government used the police to control actions and movement of people; preventing miners in one county from talking to miners from another county.

Attila the Hen

The whole thing was becoming a farce and Thatcher was being called the demented 'Attila the Hen', for as she brought in moves to prevent neighbouring miners from speaking to each other, the whole of Britain and even the world was communicating with them.

The British miners had support not only from other trades in the UK but from around the world. Solidarity sent messages of support from Poland messages of support came from Denmark and support came from the South African miners, and from Australian dockers who refused to handle coal bound for the UK.

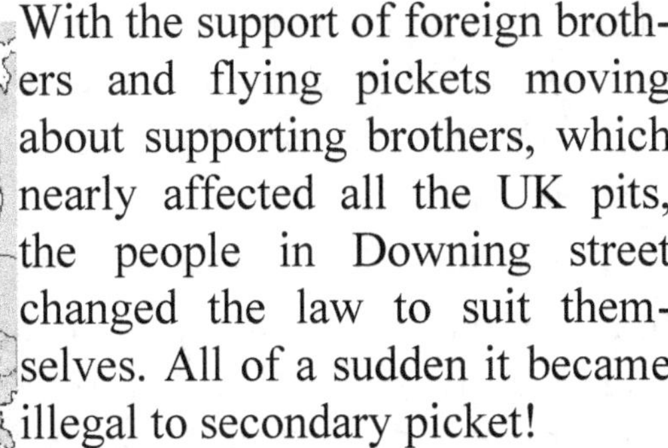

With the support of foreign brothers and flying pickets moving about supporting brothers, which nearly affected all the UK pits, the people in Downing street changed the law to suit themselves. All of a sudden it became illegal to secondary picket!

That age-old practise of supporting a fellow trade unionist against perceived bad, unhealthy or downright wrong and dangerous management practices was now suddenly against the law and the police were given orders to break up secondary picketing.

As it was difficult to know if a man was from another pit or from a factory on the picket line, some police officers appeared to think this gave them Carte Blanche to break up picket lines in general; and by actions witnessed by TV footage of the day, many seemed to enjoy their work.

In retrospect, it seems apparent that the law making it illegal to go secondary picketing enjoyed immediate support and was quickly hurried through and that could only have been possible through the actions of a similarly corrupt judiciary with the probable exception of Master of the Rolls Tom' Denning who was often seen as a supporter of the underdog.

Had this secondary picketing law have been resisted by the great power that lay in the hands of the NUM and the even greater powers of the Trades Union Congress, Thatcher and her hoard would have been broken. And the moment could never have been better as when the dockworkers struck in defence of the dock labour scheme in the July.

Thatcher was determined to get the dockers on side and get on with defeating the miners and she did, thanks to the TUC. She lied to the dockers saying the government would not "change or abolish" the dock labour scheme (which of course it did) and the dockers' leaders accepted it.

Later the pit deputies union NACODS dispute was bought off double-quick (similarly, to rebound on the deputies) by Thatcher and the Boss of the Coal Board, Ian MacGregor. Having successfully misled both the dockers and deputies, Thatcher, might have thought she was winning, at any rate, she felt confident enough to utter that disgusting and filthy statement declaring the miners to be the *"enemy within"*.

With thanks to gordonlyew.wordpress.com

That was unforgivable and had the miners had any sort of decent backing the organisers would have recognised language like that to be a clear signal of weakness and desperation on the part of the administration and not a rational government negotiating in an industrial dispute.

Therefore, the so-called *protector of the workers' rights* had to do something to demonstrate it was not in the pocket of the state. Hence, at the September Trade Union Convention, the TUC gave an undertaking that it would intervene and bring about measures to ensure solidarity to prevent the use of imported coal and oil. Yet as we know it did nothing of the kind and when the NUM lost control of its own funds and an official receiver was appointed, as history records, again the TUC did nothing to help, apparently afraid of being held in contempt of court and yet it had enormous power.

It had huge power, far more than all the courts rolled into one. It could have called a general strike and used the resources of its very clever members to prevent mail getting through, turning-off telephones, electricity and gas to Westminster and the homes of Tory MPs. It could have closed down the trouble-making Government.

In short, it could have reversed the bullying and brought Thatcher and her crew to their collective knees; but it chose to do nothing at all to help the working people who had felt they could trust and depended on it. The managing officers of the TUC did nothing to help the Miner's in their confrontation with Thatcher, However, being associated with the TUC did seem to be helpful to some.

It was extremely significant that after appearing to side with the Tories by condemning actions supporting the miners by regional TUC activists, Len Murray, top man at the Trades Union Congress received an award and became Lionel Murray, OBE, Baron of Epping Forest.

Similarly, Murray's successor, Norman Willis did nothing, he did not seem to have had room in his diary, as according to reports at the time, he was being wined and dined in the lavish home of Ian MacGregor while being lulled into preparing a document to impose on the NUM demanding an end to the strike.

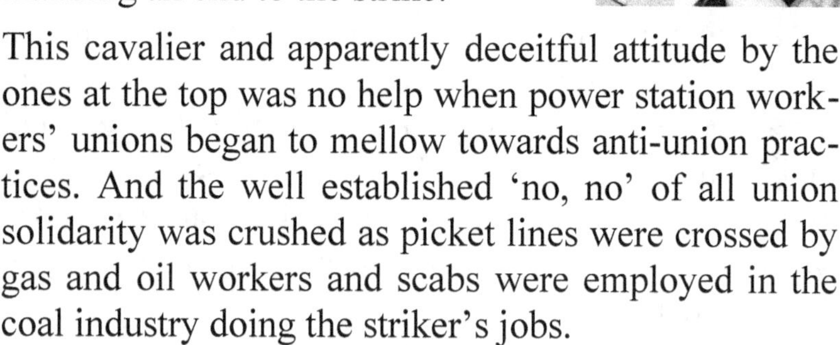

This cavalier and apparently deceitful attitude by the ones at the top was no help when power station workers' unions began to mellow towards anti-union practices. And the well established 'no, no' of all union solidarity was crushed as picket lines were crossed by gas and oil workers and scabs were employed in the coal industry doing the striker's jobs.

Nevertheless, as union officials rejected the miners and other unions began to accede to anti-union practices, the downtrodden and mistreated miners continued to be supported from abroad and by the railway workers in the UK.

Recognising this was a great deal more than just another piece of industrial action, some print workers railed against damaging cartoons and derogatory stories about central figures such as Arthur Scargill. Particularly the Sun's scathing articles and (withdrawn picture) comparing him to Hitler, which closed the paper for half the week when it refused to print an apology and a statement supporting the miners.

While the boys in blue were beating-up and charging horses into the defenceless and real mining people (people who worked in a highly dangerous industry and who were peacefully protesting about government moves that would put them out of work), Arthur Scargill tried to tell the country of the Tory's plans.

Arthur Scargill claimed to have seen a leaked paper detailing a 'hit list' of pits that were designated for closure, which Thatcher denied. Years later Arthur Scargill was proved to be the teller of truths and Thatcher the teller of lies as at the time of the strike around 75 pits were being considered for closure, putting as 

many as 35,000. *thirty-five thousand,* people out of work while the Government of the day imported coal.

"All too often miners, and indeed other trade unionists, underestimate the economic strength they have." Arthur Scargill, President of the (NUM) National Union of Mineworkers from 1982 to 2002

The effects of the 20th Century's Coal Miners' Strike of 1984/85 have remained down through the years and are still with us in the 21st Century and by all accounts will never go away; as sadly it tore families apart causing them to become bitter enemies over strikebreakers (scabs) and have never spoken to each other since.

Meanwhile, the number of pit closures have escalated and today we have 6 pits left out of 174. And from a power base of over 170,000 members in the 1980s, the National Union of Mineworkers now has less than 100 members! Talk about shooting yourself in the foot!

The miners might have lost the war but they did not lose their self-respect or the respect of the nation. And in March of 1985, with heads held high, they marched into work, every man well aware that they had alarmed Thatcher and shown her and future Tories that attacking the British worker was no easy feat.

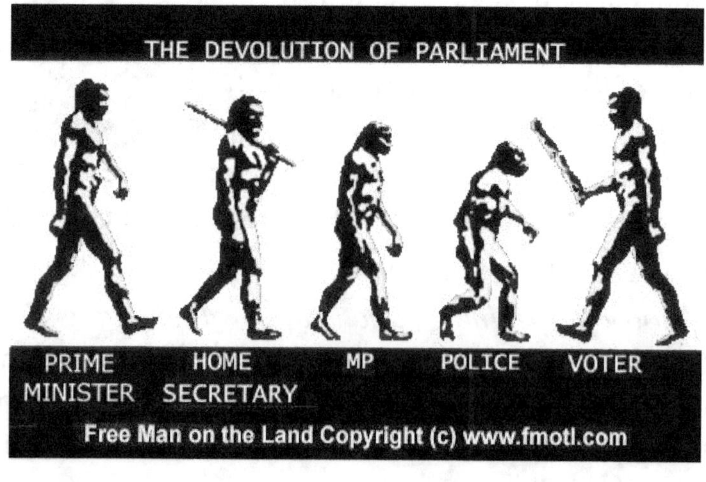

The miners taught Thatcher and any successive governments a lesson that they would be well advised to take careful notice of; and that is: you can only *bully* British people so far – and then they BITE BACK!

But it was not Thatcher or the Tories that beat the miners. It was their union and the TUC, but particularly the Trades Union Congress that shamelessly beat and destroyed the miners.

That same TUC failed to support the Firefighters during their dispute and those lads and lasses really needed help because their moralistic nature prevented them from going on an all-out strike, which the cowardly Government knew and used against them. However, again, the people recognised what a dangerous job they did and supported firefighters with money, food and clothes.

This voluntarily helping by the ordinary people is alright up to a point. But we should never forget it is organisations such as the TUC that are paid to support all trades unionists members and it must be made to recognise its responsibility and support the workers when the need arises, but if it chooses not to, *what use is it?* Therefore, is it not about time we got this, apparently, useless animal to justify its salaries and existence or tell it to go?

Addendum

Although the Coal Miners' strike of 1984–85 did happen pretty much as the forgoing has stated, in some respects, however, the miners themselves were an integral help to Thatcher's plans. I am in no way blaming the miners for the 1984/85 strike, but there was far more to the miners' industrial action than I have had space for in this little book and I would urge my gentle reader to research it in more detail.

Cartoon produced by Tony Hall, published in the Sun/News of the World 'Right of Reply Special', September 1984 © Libby Hall

Chris Butcher, "Silver Birch" grey haired miner at the Bevercotes Mine campaigned against strike.

I will say, however, that I feel in his speech, Arthur Scargill was most likely directing his words at the miners who were still working. The miners that Arthur Scargill and his successor Joe Gormley considered to be in 'safe regions' and who evidence appeared to show would have voted against a national strike.

Even so, this does not let-off the hook or in any way excuse the NUM or the TUC for their collective and disgusting behaviour for not doing all that was within their powers to help their members...

INDIRECT STATE BULLYING
Misinformation & Fraud

The controlled media working for the Tories are only able to subject people to bullying and intimidation because the majority of the people are not aware of it, having been charmed by or are hooked on one of their favourite drugs.

Karl Marks saw religion as the opium of the masses and I have to conclude that football appears to be the cocaine of the masses and together with sport in general, TV soaps, the pubs open all day, round the clock TV and box sets the majority populace is kept sufficiently anaesthetised in order that they are oblivious to government trickery taking place right under their noses. This is an extremely subtle form of *bullying* and of which examples abound, such as:

British ordnance companies selling weapons to foreign powers that are being used to kill and maim people abroad many of them children, and people getting more and more into debt due to the many TV advertisements for gambling and Bingo sites and online casinos. Then we have the bankers that are returning to paying themselves huge bonuses, having been bailed out by the taxpayer, yet still to repay those huge sums of money.

And then there are the ever-increasing power bills that pay the dividends of shareholders and pay the salaries of the fat cats from the coffers of what were public companies. The examples keep coming such as MPs giving themselves a pay rise while freezing the pay of everybody else; and that every Conservative voted against giving the health workers a reasonable cost of living pay raise and now expect those same front-line health workers to put their lives in danger to pull the Tory's fat out of the fire. And how a vote to get out of the European Union that should have happened immediately has been dragged out for over four years because the TOP will lose or not make money.

The list continues, such as how our warships are limping around on auxiliary engines because we haven't got the parts to fix the main engines. And as mentioned in an earlier book in the series, how the air force has jets that it can't just refuel in mid-air whenever the need arises because the people in the Government that we trust to run the country forgot to insist that the codes for the software be included in the price paid for the American technology. Now our air force has to pay the Americans each time it refuels one of our own jets, from one of our own tankers, in mid-air. However, there is a more sinister and immediate threat to the United Kingdom.

People are aware of the damage we are doing to our planet and the horror of a future that awaits if we don't stop misusing it. What is not generally known, however, is in the United Kingdom we have a problem with safely disposing of an amount of nuclear waste from power stations and the nuclear waste from twenty, de-commissioned, waiting to be dismantled, still containing radioactive material, nuclear submarines; I understand similar situations are current worldwide.

The radioactive submarines are being kept on private land that is costing the taxpayer hundreds of millions of pounds a year.

The really frightening thing about this situation is that it is in the hands of imbeciles. The people in charge must be idiots because, although not knowing what to do about the current poison that waits to be disposed of, they are allowing more of these horrors to be built. *Perhaps they are praying God will come up with a solution before the poison leaks?* (my italics) Source: Private Eye, edition 1385, 2015 and edition 1494, 2019.

Figuratively speaking, the Earth might be likened to a ship at sea surrounded by icebergs that threaten to inflict a 'Titanic' tear (pun intended) in the fabric of life in the coming years, but the ones in charge seem to be more concerned with making profits rather than saving our home in the cosmos.

Notwithstanding the nuclear issue, in our immediate home in the cosmos we have a pressing, personal problem to deal with, namely the current, failing well-being, of the NHS and the tricksters responsible for creating the malady, ex-Ministers for Health, Andrew Lansley and Jeremy Hunt.

The collective mischief of these gentlemen has gone largely hidden and therefore, unnoticed by the populace and is something we shall be scrutinising in the next chapter on bullying within the NHS, meanwhile, we shall continue to investigate strategies for how governments bully the public by hiding or misdirecting information.

For those people who operate out of the palace of Westminster hiding important information from the public has become an art form and is no difficult task at all when one has the might of the pet media poodles on one's side, sending up smoke screens to misdirect the public's attention from the grubby goings on.

As a thinking person, my gentle reader might wish to see for yourself what other tactics are being used to hide 'dirty tricks' in a media smokescreen.

The Revolving Door

With the ever willing assistance of the Fourth Estate, Government trickery knows no limits and borders on fraud and the best example of this is what is known as The Revolving Door. This is when an MP or a Mandarin of Westminster leaves the government to take up a lucrative post with a private company with whom s/he has been helping or giving business or advice whilst in the government post. A good example is David 'Dave' Hartnett, ex-civil servant, ex-Permanent Secretary at Revenue and Customs.

This powerful and yet unelected individual deprived the taxpayer of billions of pounds whilst at the same time apparently profiting by utilising a system that has gone on for years. In a nutshell, this is what happened. A well-known mobile telephone company receives a tax bill for over 8 billion pounds and queries it with Hartnett. Hartnett contacts the well-known phone company's accountants, one of the big four international accountancy firms. Following his conversation with the bean counters, Hartnett reduces well-known phone company's tax bill by around 7 billion pounds to less than 1.6 billion (Sweetheart Deal).

Sometime later Hartnett retires from his government post on a fat pension and it is thought he began working as a consultant for that international accountancy firms one day a week on an undisclosed remuneration package, but rumours suggest it is significant. Now isn't that a duesy? Or in the words of that famous song: It's *delicious,* it's *delightful,* it's *deloittey,* what, no, where did that come from I wonder? I think that last one is '*de lovely*'.

This writer queried the well-known phone company's tax liability in 2011 with Leslie Strathie, then chief executive at HMRC and David Hartnett's boss. In her written reply, which I still have, she stated that confidentiality *that reliable old chestnut and protective cloak of the government trickster* prevented her discussing the facts but, added the well-known phone company stated the number was an urban myth. To my knowledge, the well-known phone company has still to pay its tax bill despite selling a number of its assets worth far in access of the alleged tax demand.

The people in government that we trust to run our country are in privileged positions and, as observed, some might be tempted to abuse their responsibility for immediate personal gratification or to assist future careers, for example by way of the Revolving Door. Sadly, the temptation offered by way of this route is not the sole preserve of the Tories and I trust it is a portal that the next Labour Government will bolt, lock and weld well and truly closed.

Whether or not the next Labour leader, Keir Starmer, will do this is in the lap of the gods and as Jeremy Corbyn never had the opportunity to govern, we can only imagine. Yet, from his remarks, as a man of the people it seems apparent that it would be something that Jeremy would like to tackle. As besides enabling somebody to feather their own nests these selfish motives can result in damage or loss to the country.

I spent a good deal of my working life in the Criminal Justice System as a probation officer and I think it significant to mention that my job was instrumental in confirming my view of politics after witnessing incompetent government meddling in the probation service.

I retired some years ago, however, my friends and ex-colleagues advise me that the damage is really being felt today. Privatisation of supervision of offenders concentrates more on financial returns than the safety of the public (the probation officer's main concern) putting probation staff and the public in danger. And this is all in the pursuit of profits and when the private companies can't make profits they go into liquidation, leaving a dangerous mess of destruction in their wake.

One of the most lucrative areas for private profits from privatisation for governments has been the NHS. Over time they have gradually chipped away at the service, hiving pieces off for their paymasters to profit from. And in fact the juicy little morsel that appears to always be in the sights of the vultures is the NHS.

The Tory's attacks on the National Health Service that we have seen to date appear to be only the first tentative drafts of a horror story that promises to outdo anything Bram Stoker might have written and that brings us nicely to looking at intimidation and even corruption within the NHS.

BULLYING WITHIN THE NHS
Forcing Clinicians To Behave In Ways Possibly Life-Threatening To Patients

"The NHS Stands on a Burning Platform"

PROFESSOR MIKE RICHARDS, CHIEF INSPECTOR OF HOSPITALS

The pernicious element within Government has broken many good and honest health workers, from nurses to consultants, for telling the truth about the cost-cutting that has resulted in many deaths. And nowhere has this loss of life been more insidious than amongst the most vulnerable in society – babies and the elderly.

Ministers' meddling for profits for their paymasters is devoid of boundaries as those with power prepare the path that will take them through the revolving door on retirement from government and into a well-paid job in the private sector; a private sector company that she or he has favoured either by giving contracts, or has encouraged Government policy to favour.

Favoured policy steering and bullying within the NHS to achieve desired results grows slowly, almost imperceptibly and the two people recently instrumental in NHS policy making were Lansley and Hunt.

The Conservative, Baron Andrew David Lansley, Baron 'eh? very posh! Although still in the Tory government, movements during the EU debacle suggest that Lansley may have begun to design his career after government.

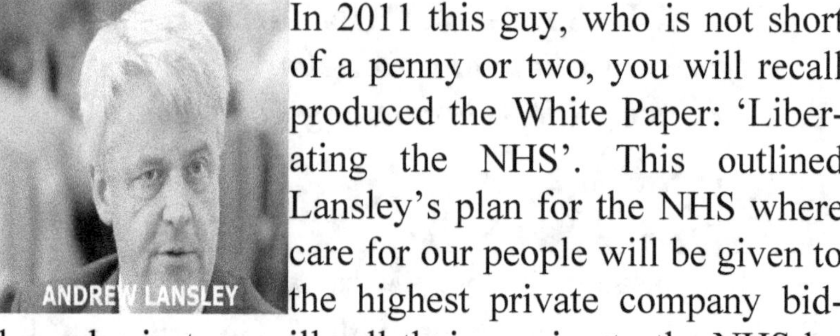

In 2011 this guy, who is not short of a penny or two, you will recall produced the White Paper: 'Liberating the NHS'. This outlined Lansley's plan for the NHS where care for our people will be given to the highest private company bidder, who in turn will sell their service to the NHS by way of GPs, whose role as medics will be deskilled and reduced to the equivalent of bean-counters as they will be solely concerned with service purchasing and balancing the books. This begs the question who will see patients and prescribe medications under Baron Lansley's Brave New World?

IS THIS HEALTH CARE IN AMERICA?

IS THIS THE FUTURE OF THE NHS?

To digress for a moment: A key part of Lansley's plan was the *Transatlantic Trade and Investment Partnership* and, which was the reason this writer voted to leave the European Union (during the fiasco disguised as democracy in 2016) as a cabal of USA, UK and European interests, the TTIP were hovering, ready to steal the NHS right from under us if we voted to remain. However, the Tory's election manifesto to leave the EU appeared to fly in the face of Lansley's plan until the Conservatives were elected and we saw that, personally, Boris Johnson wanted us to remain and the power players in charge were determined for us to remain. Now the deed has been done and we have left the EU, but have we? We have been told it was a good deal for the UK, but as the EU appears to have set the terms of the leave agreement we will have to see what happens over time. My gentle reader may wish to compare the deal with my suggestions in my last book, ***The European Union, Should We Stay Or Should We Go?***

To continue: Although RAP is not my thing, I have to hand it to the young man MC NXTGEN – real name Sean Donnelly – who says it as it is on his video, THE NHS IS NOT FOR SALE. He might not use the most eloquent of speech, but I think he has the right idea and it is time we began speaking to devious and untrustworthy people in the vernacular; they do not deserve being spoken to in respectful terms because they are not deserving of respect. Therefore, we should let them know what we, the people, who have the REAL power think of them. The following is the chant from the Rap that people on the anti-cuts demo in 2011 shouted out as they walked along... "Andrew-Lansley, Greedy-Andrew-Lansley, Andrew-Lansley, Tosser-Andrew-Lansley!"

MC NXTGEN's video can be found on the Internet on the YouTube channel as I write. However, as it might not always be there (and as I do not want to enclose a possible redundant address in my book) I would urge my gentle reader to search for Sean Donnelly's video and perhaps copy it. Perhaps it was MC NXTGEN's RAP adding to the fact that Lansley was not going down too well with the people that the *Baron* was replaced by the *Shark*.

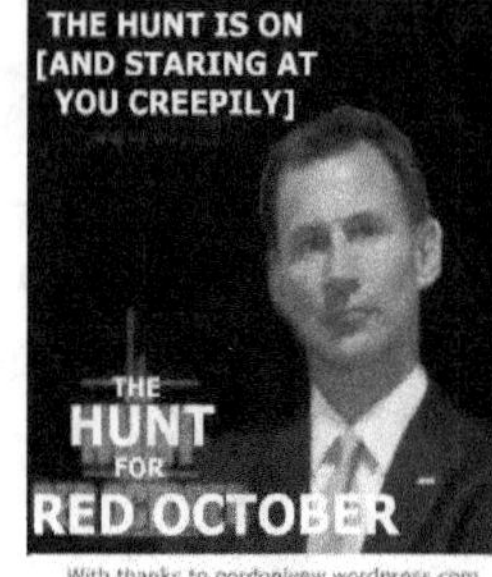

With thanks to gordonlyew.wordpress.com

Jeremy Richard Streynsham Hunt, a certain carbon-based unit whose job it was to see that the NHS functioned efficiently. Whether or not he achieved this depends from what side of the NHS bed one takes a view. Hunt did a lamentable job for the public by reducing funding and *bullying* us into accepting longer waiting lists, but this proved to be a great job for the capitalists by assisting to increase its profits; speaking of which, the Tory's have dreamed up another 'little earner' for their paymasters.

The Sustainability and Transformation Plans

The S&TPs need to be taken note of and thoroughly understood as they hold potential consequences for us all, but particularly the weakest and most unfortunate in society. In a previous book by this writer entitled: (**Homelessness Is Escalating Year After Year, Why?)** my gentle reader will find an in-depth examination of the Sustainability and Transformation Plans providing essential information and an understanding of a potentially dark future for the NHS under this latest dastardly scheme, which appears to mimic that American model.

Compact and bijou retirement home for the elderly

Under the Sustainability and Transformation Plans will we hear of, or perhaps even witness ourselves, people who are dying of cancer being turned away from hospitals because there are no beds for them, or perhaps because they cannot pay, or because of his or her age, she or he cannot get health insurance?

To underline the above. Please be very aware I am in no way blaming the hard-working medical professionals for the tragedies we hear about in our hospitals. On the contrary, I lay the blame squarely at the feet of governments past and present and, as it says above, their *arse-licking lackeys*. Hospital staff work in demanding situations while being *bullied* by administrators and other ladder-crawling toadies in various sectors *including senior clinicians*. And yet all of the hospital staff hold all of the power, the real power to make choices that will have real significance, if only they would recognise it, more of this presently.

While all the hard-working employees of the NHS diligently go about their jobs, one extremely talented young doctor, who plays the guitar and the piano has made time in his busy schedule to warn the people that the NHS is tottering on the edge of a precipice in the hands of the Conservatives. To quote Eirion Slade, "Jeremy Hunt is on a mission to destroy the NHS, and cutting doctors' pay could be the straw that breaks the camel's back." He has produced two videos to get the messages across and raise our awareness of the danger. The first is called, *Save Our Contracts* and the second is called, *The NHS This Christmas Needs You.*

I am entirely aware, as indeed I accept my gentle reader is aware that Eirion Slade's videos and songs are not new on the scene. However, although circumstances and those in power positions might have changed (Matt Hancock is the current Health Secretary as I write and Covid-19 and its various strains are putting unprecedented pressurise on the NHS), the philosophy of the Conservative party remains the same and the messages on the videos and songs are as relevant today as they ever were, probably more so.

Once again I could enclose the address of the You-Tube where Eirion Slade's videos currently reside, but powerful and devious entities might have them blocked, therefore, I would urge my gentle reader to look for and download Eirion Slade's videos and songs and spread them around.

Clinicians Afraid To Report Dangerous Practices.

Some of our young hospital professionals are quite often on their feet for unacceptable, as many as 18 (eighteen) hours continuously working a number of wards alone, especially at night.

If mistakes occur, possibly resulting in death (as a result of the clinician being worked into the ground and, totally exhausted making it virtually impossible to keep his or her eyes open, let alone prescribe drugs for patients) and they need supporting, then like rats deserting the proverbial sinking ship, those in management and others who are ultimately responsible for the Dickensian working situations – scurry away to distance themselves from the unfortunate professional.

The British Medical Association (BMA) an organisation that might be described as a union for doctors, a body that one would expect to support and protect one of their members in trouble, appears to not help them at all. The BMA is seen to turn a blind eye both to the wholly inadequate conditions doctors have to work under and watch (apparently having no scruples with being a spectator) as the General Medical Council (GMC), strikes-off the register a young man or woman who has dedicated a goodly portion of his or her life into studying to become a healer, but should we be surprised? It seems that making lots of money is more important than protecting people and saving lives.

The Scales Favour The Bully

How can mere mortals win when profits are at stake and those in charge ensure their demands are to be met by having people in powerful positions do their bidding?

It is all one big bullying club and we know this for sure when we hear of the ruler's representatives suddenly appearing at the very heart of the despicable setup, people like Charlie Massey. Charlie Massey miraculously became chief executive of the General Medical Council and apparently with nobody else being interviewed or even being considered for the post.

And the plot thickens when we learn that Massey is a stooge of Jeremy Hunt and his previous post was working closely with Hunt in the Department of Health when Hunt was the minister for Health. When a (foi) *freedom of information* request was made regarding the details of this GMC appointment, procrastination and silence there came in abundance.

It would appear, in the absence of evidence to the contrary, that Hunt managed to parachute one of his cronies into the chair of the GMC, overseeing the destruction of young medic's careers. Although Hunt's little helper is not personally responsible for the deaths of children and the elderly. It seems that Charley Massey hasn't got a clue why such things are happening and is content to accept decisions to blame junior doctors and see them struck off. Furthermore, this man in such a powerful role appears to have difficulty

putting two words together as demonstrated by his woeful ineptitude on 23rd February 2016 when trying to explain to the public accounts committee how the staffing hours and funding of the Government's 7-day NHS proposal would work.

Lorry drivers hours are capped and by law must not drive more than 10 hours in any 24 hour period, presumably, in case they lose concentration at the wheel and crash, injuring or perhaps killing somebody. That would appear to be good practise that is in place to protect not only the public but the driver him or herself and to ensure conformity with the law the police can stop a lorry driver for spot checks of documents and tachographs.

In contrast, although the European Working Time Directive appears to have limited doctors hours to 48 in any week, extrinsic evidence from GMC witch hunts suggests that junior doctors are being *bullied* into working exhaustive hours on the hospital wards, 'without declaring it' and which is putting patients' lives and young doctor's careers at risk, but with no

Bobby around to say "*'ello, 'ello, 'ello, what 'ave we 'ere den? You'd berrer take a break me, owl son,*" it's business as usual. And when anybody in the NHS tries to raise concerns, the big guns in the form of highly-paid lawyers, shut them up.

Note. *To add insult and injury to the intelligence of every man, woman and child of the United Kingdom, the House of Commons elected Jeremy Hunt into the position of chairperson on the Health and Social Care select committee. This means that Hunt has been put in a position that will enable him to be extremely instrumental (should he so chose) to obscurer or even completely obliterate any evidence of moves that he and those like him in the Tory party were responsible for that have since impacted negatively on the NHS. And as the Guardian newspaper quite eloquently put it. "The former health secretary will in effect be marking his own homework. It is bad news for the NHS, the public and democracy." Guardian online, Feb 2020.*

Gagging Those Who Try To Do The Right Thing

All attempts at *bullying* to silence people who would warn of dangerous practices within the NHS are wholly despicable to say the very least, however, what must be one of the most disgusting and dangerous incidences of *bullying* in the workplace was what happened to the surgeon, Professor Edwin Jesudason at the Alder Hey Children's Hospital in Liverpool.

Prof Ed Jesudason

The incident caused the Professor great personal distress and he made the facts of the case available in the public domain on a YouTube video. However, as with all videos on YouTube one never knows how long they will be available to view before some powerful entity has them removed. To prove and indeed confirm that observation the video of Professor Edwin Jesudason was removed. I understand this was due to some overpaid barrister convincing a court that Professor Jesudason was in breach of something or other; the fact that he was raising concerns about avoidable child deaths, did not seem to be of the slightest interest to those involved.

Barristers are extremely well paid, I understand they can command as much as £5,000 an hour and more for their time alone, but as they tend to be hired with an entourage of researches and assistants, who must also be paid, the hourly bill could run into thousands of pounds more. However, when, for example, they are retained to oversee a case lasting many months, such as that against the Professor, one could easily see the fees running into 7 figures; An enormous amount of money and who pays it? The taxpayer that is who.

This is totally wrong, but governments and local authorities get away with using public money to pay high-fee-commanding barristers to represent them in court cases where often they (the government or local authority) are in the wrong – and they hurt people. In the case of Professor Edwin Jesudason, the barrister's actions resulted in the man being made unemployed, homeless, bankrupt and penniless. But this is not over by a long way as I understand that supporters of the Professor have put up a Crowd Funding page on the Internet and many people copied the YouTube video.

 Happily, one astute member of the online community who copied the video has produced his own video concerning the 'whistleblower' case of Professor Edwin Jesudason's battle against the NHS *bullies, which* can be found on the Internet and as my gentle reader might imagine, it makes compelling watching.

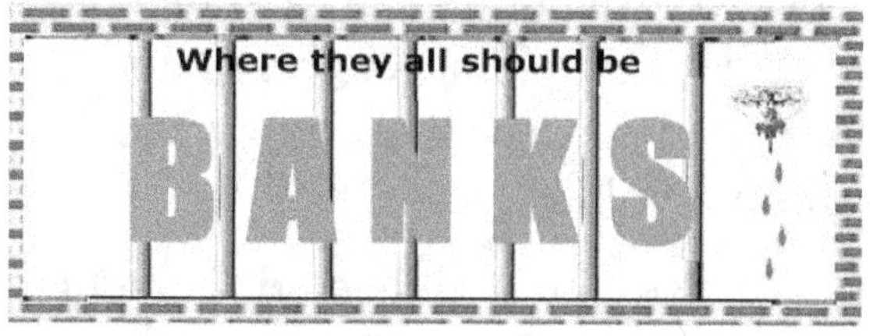

This *bullying* and putting profits first puts me in mind of a story I read some time ago about a little boy in need of a life-saving operation. He couldn't have it in this country, as the NHS would not fund it for some reason so his parents were appealing for help from the public for around £50,000 so they could take him to the USA to have the procedure. Around the same time, it was announced that the head of a bank would be paid a total of £20 million in salary and bonuses.

Is there not something fundamentally wrong here? Parents need to beg for £50,000 to save the life of their little boy whilst around the same time a man is made personally richer by the sum of £20 million; have we lost the plot completely in this country?

HEALTH WORKERS HAVE THE POWER
Paradise For The Taking

When the COVID-19 pandemic struck, the television networks encouraged the country to see the health workers as heroes, and each Thursday evening people stood on their doorsteps and saluted the NHS by clapping to show collective appreciation of the dangerous work they were doing; knowing that throughout the country people were doing the same.

The Conservative government commissioned the television coverage, encouraging every man, woman and child in the country to view the NHS workers as heroes, which is rather strange as the Conservatives have shown how lowly they consider the health workers to be.

By voting against giving the health workers a reasonable cost of living pay raise the Tories showed their contempt and derision of these people; which is beyond belief as these are the people upon whom we all depend to keep us safe, healthy and alive. And because of this these are the people who hold the real power in the country, but they will not use it even worse, they are unable to recognise it.

Yet, after years of demonstrating commitment to their vocation, in 2017 shortly after some health workers were hurt in the Grenfell Towers Fire, the Tories, to a man and woman *refused NHS staff* a meagre pay rise and it is said they even cheered when turning the health workers' claims down.

Still, in behaving the way they have during this COVID-19 pandemic, by putting the lives of complete strangers before their own, many health staff recklessly risked their own lives and the lives of their families to help the Conservatives weather, what must be the worst time to be in government for hundreds of years.

Paradise Lost!

Please Note: *this is a warning, as what you are about to read will not be seen as acceptable with a lot of people. Although, surprisingly the content was met with positive noises when it was mentioned to some doctors, nurses and maintenance staff working for the National Health Service*

Over a period of years, the Tory machine has underfunded the NHS and sold it piecemeal for-profit and plans to sell it all for profit. It has put its own people in powerful positions both in the General Medical Council and in the Health and Social Care select committee and after lording (bullying) it over the country, it is at last helpless.

A minute organism has defeated it and offered the workers of the UK the greatest opportunity to turn the tables on the Tories that any of us have ever seen and may never see again and what has been done with that precious opportunity? It has been thrown away.

The health workers' actions lost society a great opportunity to bring about a fairer and more positive method of Government by first, abandoning the Tory-favouring (First Past the Post) election process for the more fair model of (Proportional Representation); and second, taking the whole of the NHS back into public ownership and forcing Government to fund it properly and third, renationalising all privatised entities, stolen from the people.

These were such glorious opportunities, now lost and, which we may never see again for hundreds of years, if ever. The last opportunity was perhaps during William Shakespeare's time when the Black Death (plague) swept through London. And if the people then had had the modern communications we have today the likes of Shakespeare might have made the people recognise the opportunity. However, as regards today, all the anaesthetising drugs, mentioned earlier, negate the advantages, which lie largely unappreciated and so the Tories live to continue feeding off us.

Let Us Look At The Facts:

This Tory Government has a policy of selling the NHS to the private sector and has been underfunding the NHS for over ten years, therefore, it was not until the Coronavirus Pandemic struck...We discovered there was not enough medical equipment, especially ventilators, which are needed to save lives.
There were insufficient numbers of hospitals
We did not have enough doctors
We did not have enough nurses
There were insufficient numbers of ambulances
We did not have enough paramedics
We did not have enough domestic staff
There was insufficient Personal Protection Equipment

However, all of those negative points have manifested as something far worse than dealing with the Coronavirus horror alone, because the usual winter surge of, generally elderly, patients in hospitals has been overwhelmed by the need to make space for the COVID-19 sufferers, something of which the Tories did not appear to take into account in their misappropriate handling of the National Health Service.

Adding to the crisis, aeroplanes were bringing people, who might have the disease, to special hospitals in England for treatment or isolation. And although I have sympathy for those people, my priority has to be my loved ones and so I have to ask: Why bring these people, who chose to live abroad, back to the UK? Why could they not be treated where they were? And if they had to be brought to the UK, then why by aeroplane?

This choice of transport I found particularly alarming for as we all know air in a passenger carrying airliner is confined in the fuselage, *one cannot open a window at nearly one mile up in the sky.* My apologies for stressing the obvious, but the point must not be overlooked. Therefore, if a passenger/s has the COVID-19 virus, then chances are somebody on board will breathe the same air into his or her lungs and develop symptoms of the virus, including flight deck and cabin crew. Why were those people not brought by sea, surely it would have been safer for everybody? Yet, the Government allowed these people to enter the country in this manner, putting health workers lives further at risk.

As the Government were making apparently thoughtless and cavalier decisions that might well impact dangerously on the lives of health workers, what action might the health workers have taken at the outbreak of the virus? If the health workers had walked out of hospitals when the pandemic hit, what would have happened?

Thanks to PRIVATE EYE MAGAZINE

Would people have died as a direct result; well the answer to that is we don't know. However, what we do know is that lots of people have died unnecessarily throughout the years in the UK and have continued dying in large numbers since the pandemic struck as a direct result of Tory underfunding of the NHS. A doctor stated:

"An extremely high number of patients receiving critical care are needing level three care, in which they are anaesthetised and have a tube put down their throat and a ventilator takes over the work of their lungs while they are unconscious, but we don't have enough ventilators. Due to lack of proper funding of the NHS, this pandemic has caught us off guard." Source: Guardian Newspaper, September 2020.

So let us imagine that all hospital staff in all of the hospitals in the UK walked out what would happen? Well, Johnson would probably begin by running about, pulling his untamed hair out in clumps whilst convening an emergency meeting of the cabinet.

People Die – Rich People Get Richer

With his back against the wall, Johnson would need to go to the only people who could help the party, the people whose pockets the Tories have been helping to line for years and who continue to make vast sums of money during the pandemic at the expense of the people. For example, Tory donor Paul Marshall, of Marshall Wace Hedge Fund. This chap made profits of tens of millions of pounds on the stock market as the travel agent Thomas Cook went bust leaving people lamenting the loss of holidays and honeymoons. And one Tory mate of Johnson made an absolute fortune, Crispin Odey, of Odey Asset Management, made one hundred and fifteen million pounds. Source: wikipedia.org.

I would urge my gentle reader to investigate the number of wealthy people who have made billions of pounds leading up to and during the pandemic.

The Tories could not let the country see how inadequate it was, therefore, it would not want any people to die on its watch (well no more than the babies and elderly that its inadequate funding and incompetence and one-track thinking had already killed over the years, but which numbers it was able to hide).

In this event, it would need to go to those mentioned, and others it had helped become rich and ask for hundreds of billions of pounds and as they would not cough-up, we would see huge rises in council tax and every other form of tax would be hiked up and VAT would be too tempting not to be taken advantage of.

Is it possible for VAT to reach 100%, Purchase Tax did? VAT has already risen to 20%. This Cash-Cow holds the potential of putting us all into serfdom.

If we had any decent kind of representation in Westminster, rather than coming after the people who can least afford the demands for more money the Government would impose a windfall tax on everybody with a fortune of more than a million pounds the result of which would be spellbinding:

Overnight we could see more Nightingale hospitals created in every city in the UK, perhaps we would see new prefabricated hospitals emerging out of the ground on the lands of stately homes, the homes themselves might be repurposed and turned into even more hospitals and medical facilities; PPE and surgical gowns could be sourced from everywhere regardless of cost. Factories could retool to make necessary hospital equipment and vehicle factories could turn out fully equipped ambulances.

Doctors, nurses and paramedics and other medical staff would be provided with more than adequate PPE and given a good rise in pay plus being compensated for every hour worked on the wards. And consultants, used to sitting around while the young doctors did all the work, could be forced to return to generic hospital duty. Furthermore, we might see doctors and other medics, attached to the armed services, command-eered into civilian hospital service.

We would see the tables turned on bullying as the health workers laid down the rules. The health work-ers would agree to work on condition that the Govern-ment conceded to the people's demands first. And those would be instigating proportional representa-tion, the NHS back to public ownership and a pro-gramme of renationalisation. All the things the Tories would hate. All of the above demands would be in writing with clauses to protect them from any future government of either colour from ever trying to over-turn, alter or overrule them.

Because of the health workers and their unfailing ded-ication to duty and commitment to saving lives my gentle reader might feel that glorious opportunity would appear to have been lost for all time, but on the contrary, it is not completely beyond recall as we shall see.

It might be argued that the health workers were heroes for selflessly going into hospital, risking their lives to save the lives of strangers and I would not disagree that their actions probably did have positive out comes. However, I would argue that their actions had the effect of being a two-edged sword, which the Government was too well aware of and used to its own advantage.

On first thought, the health workers' actions would appear right and seem to make sense. However, things that seem to make sense are not always right and one needs to think, investigate and research before making one's mind up and coming down firmly for or against a motion.

Were medics who went into work with inadequate personal protection heroes and did they improve the situation or not? Whilst it cannot be denied that medics saved some lives, there is an argument that causes one to feel that overall, things might have been better had the medics stayed away from work until the Government had agreed to the terms mentioned. To this my gentle reader might be thinking, how could this be? And the answer is quite clear when one has all the pieces of the puzzle.

You will not read what I am about to say in the Daily Mail or Express or any other Tory-supporting newspapers. But it seems that not all health workers were foolish enough to sacrifice themselves and their families for the Tory's cause. Eavesdropping on conversations between receptionists in medical establishments revealed that many doctors, nurses and other National Health Service staff chose to stay away and it might be that in staying away they actually saved lives.

The reasons are, fewer people to spread the virus (nurses are known to wear their uniforms shopping in supermarkets). Fewer people demanding scarce PPE resources. Not being totally sure about procedures because we were receiving inadequate information from

Government and no clear guidance from the professionals, which, suggested that the boffins, if not exactly lying and deliberately misleading us, appeared to be making up the rules as they went along and were keeping us very much in the dark – or as I overheard somebody on a bus say: *they were winging it!*

It is probably a reasonable hypothesis to deduce that the death toll caused by the COVID-19 virus would have been greatly reduced, with a full complement of NHS staff saving lives, but only with everybody feeling it was completely safe to come into work for both themselves and their families and that situation would have been the case…

(1) If the National Health Service had been adequately funded over the years. (2) If governments had planned for worst-case scenarios, ensuring that enough hospitals and hospital beds were available regardless of time of year. (3) If hospitals had adequate supplies of up-to-date equipment. (4) If hospitals had adequate supplies of personal protection equipment for every member of staff. (5) If governments had ensured that every health authority in the country was equipped with an adequate and healthy fleet of modern ambulances. (6) And if enough doctors, nurses and paramedics were trained each year.

In view of our observations I feel I have no choice but to lay the blame for all of the deaths caused by the COVID virus, squarely at the door of Conservative Governments, past present and (if experience is anything to go by) in the future.

Food For Thought

During the 9/11 horror when the hijacked aircraft were flown by suicide bombers into the Twin Towers in New York City killing hundreds of innocent people, both inside the airliners and in the buildings I understand that the people responsible made lots of money on the Stock Market, which although despicable, was perhaps understandable from their point of view.

What was by no means understandable from any point of view and in no way acceptable and was quite certainly the very height of despicable, was that lots of other people made lots of money and some made millions out of the deaths of those innocent people. Similarly, during the current COVID-19 pandemic, which has caused the deaths of countless people around the world, lots of people made lots of money and some made lots of millions.

We don't know for certain, but given their track record (the Tories and their friends were probably amongst the other people who made millions out of the horror of 9/11, all off the backs of dead people). But what we do know for certain is that Tory donors made millions during the pandemic off the backs of dead people.

We also know the Tories are fawning over our wonderful health workers and are using them to cover the Tories own failings and inadequacies, but really see them as low life and will in all probability return to treating the workers of the National Health Service as such when we are out of the threat posed by this pandemic. Meanwhile the Tory machine is like a giant turtle that has been put on its back and cannot get back up and this is the time to drive a spear through its heart! Therefore, this is a clarion call to our health workers to revisit the power position you hold and use it to pay back the Tories…

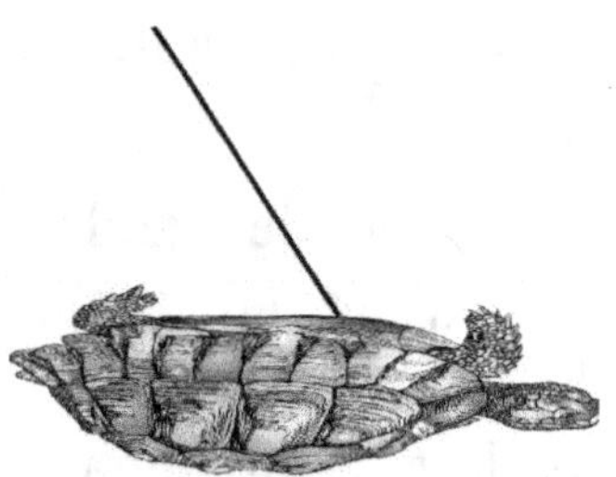

…if only for the way they treated the honest and hard-working miners and remember the words of Arthur Scargill,

"All too often miners, and indeed other trade unionists, underestimate the economic strength they have."

REMEMBER THIS HEALTH WORKERS YOU HOLD ALL THE CARDS!

BULLYING BY STEALTH

Subliminal Messaging And
Intimidating The Unconscious Mind

The Charity Business In The 21ˢᵗ Century.

I would ask my gentle reader to always keep in mind that bullying can take on many disguises, for example, take charities! Are they entities with good and honest motives or really good money-making scams?

An object of coercion that largely passes by un-noticed, because the majority of us are willing to help somebody in distress, is the charity shop. People tend to take unwanted goods to a charity shop, this is be-cause we have been subliminally conditioned to think that way. Why not sell the goods and give the money to those you want to help, at least they will get it all?

Are those who work voluntarily in charity shops cheating somebody out of paid work? If previous charity shops were to reopen as retail outlets they would provide people with salaried employment.

It used to be thought that if people chose to work in charity shops for no pay that was their choice, but atti-tudes are changing. Individuals, who for years, have been willing to work in charity shops for no financial reward thinking they were helping unfortunate people are beginning to realise that others are profiting greatly off their selfless work. One person I spoke to working in a well-known charity organisation's shop had the following to say:

"I heard we got special low rents, but my sister told me something she'd seen on the Internet that shocked me. We have directors that get paid good wages with cars and all kinds of other things." (Recorded verbatim with the person's authority to print, provided she remained anonymous)

In order to hide information likely to be damaging, Government will put up smokescreens, meaning snippets of information designed to take one's mind away from the information. It might be a serious issue inducing anger or it might be complete nonsenses designed to make one dismiss it with derision. It really does not matter how it is met with by the public, the whole idea is that it occupies one's mind.

For example, some time ago, we were all subjected to the EU hokum of whether or not prisoners should have the right to vote. What riveting food for thought. Gee whizz! Now, what would they use their vote for, perhaps they might put in a *dishonest Government?* Now wouldn't that make a change?

The likes of that complete nonsense is a smokescreen to hide some tricky, underhand and possibly unlawful activity on the part of the government of the day and we need to see through these distractions and understand they are unimportant and **THEY DO NOT MATTER.**

This nonsense will be played on by the Tory's gutter press *we have seen what that is* and, which will purposely obscure news that is likely to lose votes for the Tories, for example…

...refusing a life-saving operation for a child and the head of a bank being paid a total of £20 million in salary and bonuses; more money than ordinary people would earn in ten lifetimes.

What does matter is the hatchet job Thatcher and successive governments have done to the *National Health Service, Post Office, Telephones, Education, Gas, Electricity, Water, Airlines, Coal Mines, Trains, Buses* and just about anything else that wasn't nailed down in the UK.

On the subject of powerful organisations in the hands of the privateers, although already in private hands we must not forget the banks – and the alarming words of warning of Thomas Jefferson:

[...] If the people ever allow private banks to control the issue of their currency, the banks will deprive the people of all property... The issuing power should be taken from the banks and restored to the people, to whom it properly belongs.... I believe that banking institutions are more dangerous to our liberties than standing armies [...] Thomas Jefferson (1743 – 1826) American lawyer and Founding Father, third president of the United States. Author of the Declaration of Independence and a proponent of democracy who motivated colonists to break from the United Kingdom.

These essential services, including Building Societies and the Banks, should not be in the hands of privateers. The revenues generated belong back in the system to keep and create jobs and make the services better for the people, but the profits go into the coffers of the privateers or should that be Pirates and their speculative shareholders who tend to be wealthy people? Therefore, my gentle reader, how was the selling-off of state industries into private hands accomplished? Well quite subtly actually. Thatcher and her cohorts advised that everybody could buy shares in the new British companies knowing full well what would happen.

Here follows an example from the time: Remember, in the 1980s, the television announcements pronouncing: *'Tell Sid, British Gas shares are worth a packet'?* The name Sid was a patronising piece of subliminal advertising as it seemed to be speaking to the ordinary man, appearing to say that the sell-off was in his interest, that he could buy shares and be part of the new world. And yes, he could buy shares, a few because he did not have a great deal of money to buy them in any meaningful numbers. And then having bought them he pretty soon sold them off for a pitiful profit and thought he had done well, but it was all part of the plan.

The wealthy hoovered up the shares in their thousands as soon as they came back onto the market and that is how the wealthy are steadily coming to own our country and these are lessons we should learn well. These are the important things and **THESE DO MATTER.**

Before moving on I am reminded of a further Government's pet media's smoke screens a couple of years ago. It was suggesting moves to put ethnic minority's pay in parity with whites. What, were they saying that black people were paid less than white people for doing the same job? *No of course not* – this was another diversionary tactic.

There are many things that are wrong in our society of which the pet media poodles do not need to tell us and of course would not tell us, but which do need to be dealt with. Top of the list is the NHS, which we need to ensure is rock steady, then we can deal with everything else that is rotten in the 'State of Britain'.

To put the observations of the previous paragraphs into a nutshell: The United Kingdom has been steadily stolen in stages from us the people and the taxpayers and it continues to be stolen, piece by piece, enabling some very wealthy people to become even wealthier. And what do we do about it...?

...We Work For Nothing!!!

If you drive a school bus for nothing, if you work in a charity shop; if you organise people to clean-up beauty spots, rivers, parks and the like; if you do anything for nothing then you are doing somebody out of a paid job. And you are a big part of the problems we have today!

Remember this: If it needs doing it needs being paid for, or to paraphrase a well known literary figure: *"No man but a blockhead ever worked except for money"* Dr Samuel Johnson, (1709-1784).

What he actually said was: *"No man but a blockhead ever wrote except for money"* (well that's told me), but the sentiment is exactly the same. *And that advice came out of the mouth of a Tory, which just goes to show that Conservatives do not work for no pay.*

So what this man is telling us is: If you arrange events or compete in them, if you are a volunteer in any capacity whatsoever then, regardless of your good intentions, if you are not being paid you are a blockhead. Furthermore, you are adding to the misery in this country and, as stated above, the more you volunteer the more you become part of the continuing cause of our problems.

If that seemed a bit harsh, consider the case of the little boy needing the life-saving operation. His parents appealed for cash as well they might, but why should they need to? Because the money we pay in taxes to help this little boy is both being stolen, and wasted on all manner of scams and useless things by a Government that knows *people's heartstrings* will be tugged and the people will come to the aid of the little boy. But let's back off, put aside emotion for a moment and consider what is really happening here.

We Are Being Played Like A Piano!

We go to work to earn our living, out of which we pay an amount in tax, We buy our weekly shopping and we pay tax, we pay our phone bill and we pay tax and now VAT (Vile Autocratic Theft) as well; we top-up the car, more tax and VAT; we tax and insure our car and more well… tax and VAT. We buy our children presents and we pay more tax and still more VAT. And that is just for starters, the things that are visible and obvious, there are lots of sources of taxation that are not so obvious.

All of this tax goes to the government in power, which is expected to use the money collected from all taxes to see every aspect of our country runs as smooth as clock-work. When added up, the taxes we pay are enormous and far and away more than enough to meet the needs of everybody in the country. If my gentle reader has not thought about this before I am sure you are getting the idea now. *"Out of every pound we earn, we end up with 37p." Source:* Which online, 2018.

The rest goes to Government one way or another. and what do they do with it? They don't run the railways, privateers look after that. They don't build hospitals and schools; Private Funding Initiatives (PFIs) look after them. PFIs, a monster monetary policy used by governments of both parties are a whole new can of worms that promise a sinister future for our children.

As nothing remains nationalised, thanks to Thatcher and Milton Friedman and his Chicago school of economics, the government really do not do anything when one thinks about it. Sitting on their collective bums, they let their mates run the country, hiving-off the profit and they even give it a catchy name: it's called *Rolling Back The State*.

Rolling Back the State

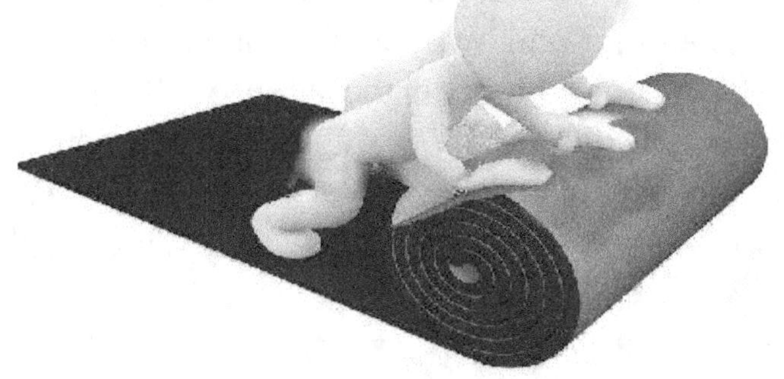

Still, we pay our taxes and accept it when they say there is no money to fund that child's life-saving operation or there is no money to buy the medicine to keep another child alive and out of pain. That's not good enough! *That is why I pay my taxes!*

I want my taxes to help save that little boy's life and all the other children who are seriously ill. I want my taxes to pay for the expertise and medications to *treat and cure sick children and the elderly people* in this country. I don't want my taxes to pay for arms to *create sick and dead children and sick and dead elderly people* in foreign countries.

Dr Johnson Is Saying Stop Working For No Pay!

But wishing and talking alone is not going to change anything, something far more direct will be needed, perhaps we could take a leaf out of the Capitalist's book and turn the tables on the government and defeat it, but how would we fair?

Imagine for a moment if people refused to work in charity shops, drive vehicles, clean up beauty spots and organise events to raise money to save lives for no pay, what would happen? Would drug and alcohol organisations fold? Would children suffer, would they die? Would adults suffer, would they die? Would disabled people be stuck indoors all day? Would hospices be forced to put dying, elderly people out on the streets?

No, that most certainly would not happen as, collectively, we provide enough money to support everything in this country. However, I do know that if one person died, due to inadequate government management, it would be the *people* who would get the blame. Yes, the *people* and they would be blamed by the government who would be sent into a tailspin that they would need to control to get things back to the way they were – and so the government would do whatever was required to achieve this.

Although the 'powers that be' will appear to acknowledge the people's argument, proclaiming from the rooftops, (*No Pay, No Work. Something that needs to be done is by nature a job of work providing employment and should therefore, be paid as such*) However, it will just be patronising 'Newspeak' and behind the scenes, a powerful team of government tricksters will be hard at work orchestrating a strategy to defeat the people.

Those in charge would not hesitate to use public money to commission large billboard images, carefully crafted depicting the people as cruel and uncaring, together with carefully, negatively worded messages on posters and in magazines and newspapers and on Internet webpages reflecting those negative images of the people as being insensitive and selfish. The Government would even send carefully crafted letters to every household in the United Kingdom, regardless of the cost, accusing us of being heartless, cruel, merciless and uncaring and every other negative it could come up with to make us feel as though we were cold-hearted bastards.

Copyright © 2018 Private Eye

Compounding its onslaught would be the broadcasting media, which besides providing a captive market for the capitalist's advertisements the television set has become an ideal weapon… er… instrument for getting to the hearts of the people in their own living rooms at home. Thus with well-known actors broadcasting the government's messages (by forcing fake emotions, *which is easy for them as they lie for a living),* the government would get back to having the common person grease the wheels of their gravy train again.

Having regained its position as the big charity 'begging bowl, the television set would recommence its mischief, using more actors and so-called celebrities to encourage us to be generous and giving (many of whom are extremely wealthy and can easily afford to be altruistic) whenever the contenders in the annual round of solicitation is approaching, for example the Red Nose Day appeal.

Red Nose day being an appeal for money to send to African villages to help save injured people's lives, some of whom are suffering from the result of armed conflicts in their country. Armed conflicts, for which *British companies likely provided the ordnance* and were financed by the likes of that banker we spoke of earlier and his cohorts. But we'd be depicted as the bad guys in all of this because we would be refusing to work for nothing or give any longer to charities.

Members of the public might even be subjected to nuisance telephone calls advising: if they agreed and supported the movement for N*o Pay, No Work* then they are bad people who will be punished.

Religious leaders would add their weight to the *bullying* of the people and undoubtedly the pressure would be relentless and would continue and people would begin to believe government propaganda supported by those celebrities and religious figures again appealing to our sense of decency to help the sick and dying. And blame and insults will be levied at those who try to stick it out until government has the whole thing back under its control and we get back to the way things were. Then friends of the government will return to getting their huge perks, bankers will again get their huge salaries and bonuses and cabinet ministers and the mandarins of Westminster will continue dishing out lucrative contracts to organisations who will employ them on huge salaries when they leave government through the Revolving Door; and we'll all be coerced into working for nothing again.

Charity Shops Have An Unfair Advantage

In my view, which is backed up by speaking to many people, charities, in general, are getting out of hand and new charity shops are popping up all over the place. At one time we recognised the few charity shops on the high street, but now all manner of unfamiliar names are opening up in shop premises that were once occupied by businesses, businesses forced to close due to…err...*lack of business; ironic don't you think?*

Charity shops in general appear to be losing sight of who they are and where they stand in the order of things. The prices they are charging for used goods that they acquire for free is becoming unreasonable and people have been heard to remark they are able to buy new items cheaper in markets and high-street outlets.

I have been informed by a market trader that charity shops are becoming hated by his colleagues as they are presenting the store holders with an unfair advantage. He advised me that charity shops pay no or very little rent and rates, okay council tax, but a *rotten rose by any name still smells as putrid* (sorry Will'); and from the stock, which they get for nothing, only a small percentage has to go to the named charity.

I have no reason to doubt what our friend tells me and in fact, my investigations into the larger ones, quite difficult given their secretiveness, would seem to add credence to his claims as the picture is quite alarming (and as previously mentioned) involving large salaries, expense accounts and company cars and all paid for by the generous donations *freely given by the downtrodden,* good-hearted, but taken for fools working people.

The downtrodden people are even being stopped in the street and practically coerced into giving to this or the other. And this is especially wrong to people of little means who have been made to feel bullied and embarrassed into giving money that they can ill afford to part with. However, taking the good-hearted people for fools does not end there. It is one thing when a wealthy banker, company executive, cabinet minister or business woman or man smirks on television, saying something similar to the following:

They asked me, so I was happy to do my bit for charity. I helped clean out the local river and now the fish are returning.

That is fine as they can easily afford to do it. However, it is quite something else entirely when a young penniless and out of work person with no hope of improvement is embarrassed into working for nothing.

Charity Begins At Home'

The whole charity thing puts me in mind of when I was a youngster and I remember the older and wiser members of my family saying, they pay their taxes for the government to take care of things and would quote the old adage that *'charity begins, **and ends**, at home'*.

Government assumed the mantle of running this country we didn't ask for it. We pay our excessive taxes and expect those who have won the competition to govern – to do just that. It should not expect people to work for nothing to subsidise the Capitalists' profits, which is exactly what is happening when people involve themselves in charity work.

Should my gentle reader still not be convinced of the subtle bullying going on all around I would urge you to check how much money government friends owe in unpaid corporation tax, VAT and income tax, i.e. that well-known phone company for a start, but there are many more.

Perhaps the time has come to take a fresh look at charities and tell the multinationals, who make huge profits by causing wars and destroying countries, to dig deep and use those profits to help the people and fix the damage, which they, the multinationals are responsible for causing in the first place? We, the people of this country have better things to do, like ensuring we are able to care for our own families with the small amount of earned income that the Government condescends to allow us to keep.

In concluding this observation of things that are un-equal in our society and how we are *bullied* by those we deem to be more powerful than us. I would urge my gentle reader to recall the words of Arthur Scargill. Remember Arthur said, "*All too often miners, and indeed other trade unionists, underestimate the economic strength they have.*"

You, the ordinary, honest and hard-working person with a well-balanced sense of decency and a wish to see all people treated fairly hold the real power if only you would remember that and ignore Tory propaganda and stick together; in this event we might paraphrase Arthur Scargill's words as:

"*All too often the people underestimate the economic strength they have.*" And if my gentle reader has any difficulties picturing how this might be, I'll leave you with the following vision.

When we understand this is how it works, and not the other way around, we'll have found the beginning of a solution to our problems

EPILOGUE

We began our observations by noting that both Capitalism and Nature appear to function through cruelty and intimidation.

Adequate evidence for this hypothesis seemed to arise from how, at times, both human animals and wild animals present as extremely cruel and sometimes downright heinous in their behaviour towards their own species.

The difference between cruel bullying and non-academic discipline was then considered and we noted what at first seemed to be deplorable and vicious treatment by wild animals to their own kind, was really the manifestation of hundreds of thousands of years of imprinted disciplined behaviour largely keeping members safe, individually and as a whole.

With the understanding that wild animals work together based on an unyielding discipline that helps the group, it did not take a great leap to appreciate that the people behind Capitalism will help themselves to anything, at any cost to people or the planet and this is made to work due to bullying.

With bullying firmly in our sights we examined other forms of intimidation happening all around us, sometimes barely noticeable as bullying. And we appreciated that bullying is endemic in society, it begins aggressively in school and builds virtually unobtrusively throughout one's life.

The gas and electricity demand, the overdrawn bank statement and the late mortgage payment reminder are all written forms of the genre, intended to intimidate one into behaving a certain way. Today, however, Information Technology has brought into our lives a much swifter and targetted method of bullying.

It would seem that the old adage of, *sticks and stones may break my bones but, words will never hurt me*, needs to be consigned to the annals of history as words can do everything actions can, as evidenced by the hurt caused by so-called 'cyber-bullying' and, which has been known to be the cause of suicide between young people.

Moving on, we saw that governments lie and defraud the country by using tax money inappropriately. And we saw they are masters at deception, leading people, directly and indirectly, to behave in certain ways. And we noted how they use strategies to achieve their aims, such as labelling their quarry either by humiliating or viciously attacking it or them and then misinforming the public by sending up smokescreens to cloud the issues, with the assistance of their pet media acquaintances.

We have seen the bullying taking place in the NHS and how good and caring people who dedicate their lives to helping others have had careers destroyed just for raising concerns. And we have seen how the bullies protect their positions by putting cronies in powerful positions to ensure profits at the expense of lives.

We have discussed all of those things in the pages of this book and if my gentle reader is anything like me you will have began noticing other things that tend to pass us by. For example, recently I heard of somebody receiving a warning letter for falling behind with the regular payments concerned with the individual's house, not the mortgage payments, but the ground rent (it seemed that some large corporation owned the ground that this person's house stood upon).

While I was writing I could not help pondering on that person's predicament, which caused me to think of our own house. Although our house is not leasehold, we own it and the land, still, I began to think… how can anybody own land? I mean it is the Earth, how the hell can you legitimately own a piece of the World?

At one time during the process of buying a building, the buyer's solicitor would want to see the conveyancing papers, which were obtained from the Government's Land Registry Office. The conveyance papers contained a list of the owners of the property going back many years, but like so many things, that has all changed.

In the Tory's rush for profits, the Land Registry Office was sold to the private sector and the conveyance papers are no longer a part of the process. Instead, every house in the UK is now what is called *registered*. This is helpful in speeding up the selling processes, but it really is too bad with regard to the buying part of the process, because now the list of past owners is no longer made available. I imagine they could be requested from the Land Registry, but this would no doubt be time-consuming and would probably involve a fee, which at one time was free.

When we bought our current house, around thirty-five years ago, solicitors were charging a good deal of money to do what the people in the Land Registry Office showed me was so simple, that I did the conveyancing work myself. In fact, I performed every aspect of the house buying process and saved a fortune in so doing. Like everybody else, we had fully intended to use the services of the professionals for all aspects of the work, but we could not afford their fees. That's it, I was not trying to be clever, we just did not have the money.

I documented my house buying experience, which my gentle reader can freely download in ebook form. The details are at the front of this book.

I spent many hours needlessly pouring over Land Law books before I discovered that the Land Registry would tell me whatever I needed to know. However, my times in the library were not totally wasted as it was during those quiet times that I began to notice how much we are all bullied and hence, the seeds of this book were sown.

Upon examining the conveyancing papers documenting the previous owners of our intended house, I noted that the process ended when the house was built in 1939 and before that, nothing! I imagined how the piece of land that the house was standing on could lawfully be the property of the first-ever owners and of course, it could not, as it was *stolen.* In common with every other piece of the Earth, it was purloined by bullies who told the people they had been chosen by God and were the Devine rulers of the Earth and so had the right to the land.

The people, being ignorant peasants who were so terrified of the awesome power over life and death these thieves wielded, they accepted the land owner's assumed rights. But that was then and this is now and we are not ignorant peasants any longer. We have intelligence, we can think for ourselves and we can use reason and we should use those attributes to bring about a fairer world, a world were bullying, intimidation, coercion and domination by one individual or group over another has been dispatched to the waste bin of history for all time.

One For All And All For One, Young D'Artagnan

People, especially young people, tend to hate the concept of Communism, seeing it as something loathsome, wrongly in my view. Therefore, I began asking clients what the word meant to them. Unsurprisingly, most reacted unfavourably, the following being an overview of thought:

A political state where governments forbid opposition to its rule, exercising extreme control over all activities.

When advised that was more '*Totalitarianism*', which enemies of '*Communism*' often spout, and that the true spirit of Communism is a society advocating:

*equality for all, a society structured on common own-
ership of the means of production, which looks out for
everybody in a social, political and economic system
without social classes or government interference.*

When clients heard this they were more inclined to
agree that Communism did not seem like such a bad
thing after all, and thought to begin working to rid society of bullying it is what we should be striving for.
But to be able to do this in a society where we still
have the descendants of those who lived off our ancestors, continuing to live off us and being protected,
we seem to be handicapped.

It is not just in this country either, throughout the
world the bullies are protected by the two Rs: Rank
and Religion. Only when the Fantasy destroys the
Myth will people be free or as a wise man once said:

*"Men Will Never Be Free Until The Last King Is
Strangled With The Entrails Of The Last Priest."*
French Atheist Denis Diderot (1713-1784):

Some argue Diderot did not say this. I am not concerned who said it, It is the inspired sentiment that
counts for me.

And as regards the ownership of land, the North
American indigenous population have a lovely attitude to the Earth. They believe:

"The Earth Does Not Belong To Us
We Belong To The Earth."

POEM BULLYING

We start out in life an accident
that's how we're born on Earth.
With traits locked in a blueprint
that shapes our path from birth.

This means there is no difference
with the tramp and engineer.
For neither had a choice of whose
DNA they'd be the heir.

And life is similarly balanced,
not resulting in fair measure.
For privileged ones will steal
and cheat adding to their treasure.

From atop their lofty places
they trick the weak and poor
with junk TV and football
and the pub's all-day open door.

So our post in life is set at birth
and favours rich and strong.
And bullying begins in school
and lasts our whole life long.

So why are we surprised to hear
strong children hurting weak?
For this is life's cruel legacy,
it's a template for the meek.

If born in wealth and privilege
then good life will be assured.
And you'll live your life in luxury,
need and poverty obscured.

Your existence was pure chance
so if born poor in this real lottery,
then chances are you'll be the prey
for all of your earthly entity.

Good fortune may present itself
and prospects you may find
and if keen of brain and
quick of wit and studious of mind...

...then you will have the basic tools
to help prosper and to lift
you from the ranks of those of whom
were not born with your gift.

For those who life has failed to give
good minds, it might instead,
give bodies strong with which to make one's way
and earn one's bread.

But those who life has failed to give
keen minds or strong physique,
will go through life deprived and poor
powerless to find their niche.

These are the ones that life visits
so harshly and so cruel.
They're tormented by their peers,
at play and within school.

And then within the workplace,
the system and bureaucracy.
These people have no where to turn,
for help to hear their plea.

Nature's indifferent to their plight,
it cares not for their pain.
It wants procreation of the race,
so the best of us remain.

And it seems endemic on this planet
that tyranny must always rule.
And those with power will use it
as an all prevailing tool.

As strong animals prey on the frail
and kill the weak for food,
strong countries wage war on those
they know will be subdued.

And in this quest the young are killed
on both sides from the poor,
reinforcing that, which we know is fact,
oppression's at the core.

So listen to me world oppressors
as this song for you is meant,
why wage war, bomb weak and poor
and cause them all torment?

And to all the bullies of the weak
why hurt folk, it's perverse?
When our precious life is but a flash
in this great universe!

Copyright eam © 2000

I don't know what my gentle reader thought about the poem, It is all my own work and was not that easy to produce so I have a new respect for writers of verse.

Anyhow, it does have a serious message, which needs to be heard. Therefore, sophisticated or naive, please copy and spread it around (together with the videos of Eirion Slade and indeed the other videos mentioned).

My copyright notice is due to legal advice but, the verse is mine to do with as I wish; all that is required is that the copyright notice is kept.